HOW TO DO EVERYTHING
WITH
MARKERS

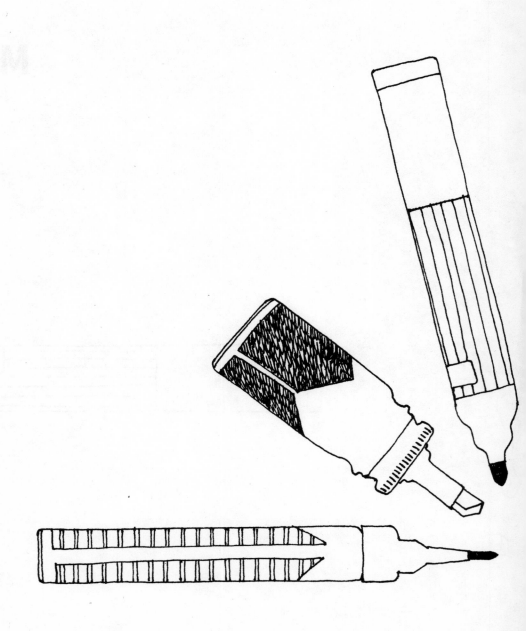

HOW TO DO
EVERYTHING
WITH
MARKERS

by
Laura Torbet

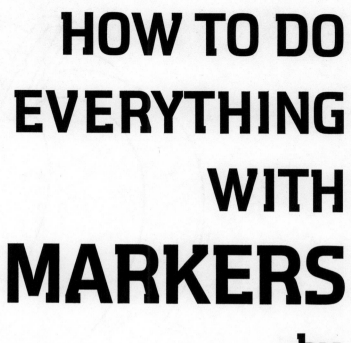

BOBBS-MERRILL
INDIANAPOLIS
NEW YORK

Designed by Tom Torre Bevans
Manufactured in the United States of America

First paperbound printing, 1978

Library of Congress Cataloging in Publication Data
Torbet, Laura.
    How to do everything with markers.
    1. Felt marker decoration.   I. Title.
TT386.T67   745.7   76-4169
ISBN 0-672-52143-1
ISBN 0-672-52531-3 Pbk.

HOW TO DO EVERYTHING
WITH
MARKERS

CONTENTS

CLOTHES AND ACCESSORIES

THINGS FOR CHILDREN

ALPHABETS

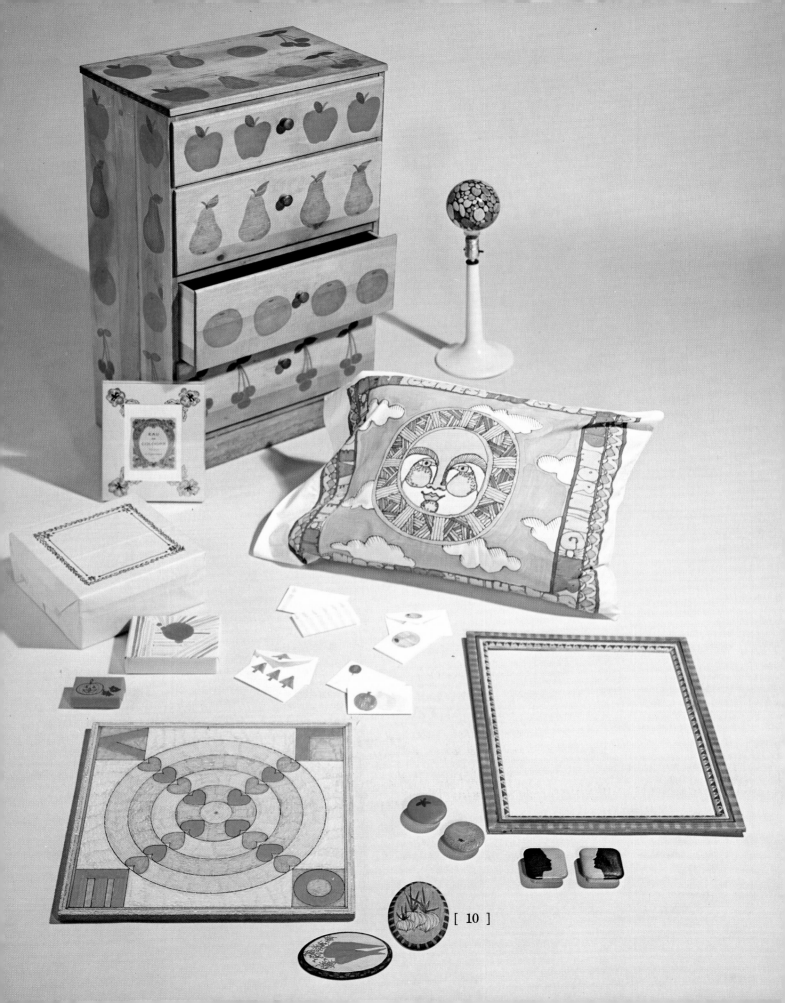

16

I love my markers. Of all the mediums I've worked with, markers are my first love. They are easy to use and quick to produce results; they come in endless and dazzling colors, and they are versatile in their applications. Dabbling in many crafts as I do, it seems as if there is always a new use for markers, always something new to try.

This book is about the many, many things you can do using markers as your basic tool—on everything from wood and plastic to fabric and paper. The investment in a set of permanent markers is minimal, and their uses seemingly infinite. For me, they are unique, because they "accomplish the job"—that is, they get results quickly, easily and without additional equipment, or extensive preparation, finishing or cleanup. You don't have to be facile with a brush and paints or be an accomplished needleworker to produce professional-looking work, as you can with markers.

There are so many things you can do with markers to turn the most plain, pedestrian item into a thing of glory. Just about anything can be markered, and many times the most mundane things turn out quite spectacular, with a minimum of effort. Entire transformations can occur with markers. A markered pillowcase makes a very decorative throw pillow. Curtains become room dividers. Old sheets become Halloween costumes.

Then, too, markers are often the answer as to what to do with a piece of clothing, a bedspread, a leather purse, which is stained or has become dingy with wear. You can rejuvenate many things and give them a whole new, and different, life.

This book contains complete instructions for prettying up anything from furniture to clothing, to kitchen and household items, gifts and party decorations. Because of the ease of working with markers not everything you do has to be a lasting monument. A markered Parson's table, of course, will last forever, but while you'd never take the time to embroider "Happy 16th Birthday, Susan" on a set of napkins, you would *spend half an hour* or so to marker a one-dollar T-shirt, or a set of paper napkins and tablecloth, or a special gift wrap. "Throwaway" projects are a marker forte. And markers also have hidden talents in such areas as repairs on various materials, personalized items and gifts.

And of course kids and markers are a natural combination. Their clothes and furniture are small, so it is easy to work on projects for children, and the bright marker colors lend themselves well to children's motifs. Kids also love to work with markers—they're colorful and easy to handle. Any child old enough to keep things out of his mouth, and careful enough to replace the caps after using, is old enough to use markers. If you have toys or clothes which are the worse for wear, let your children marker them. There are several projects in this book which are suitable for children to work on. Let a sick child marker a pillowcase for his sickbed. At a party, buy a bunch of boys' cotton knit undershirts, and let each child marker his own T-shirt. Let them try their own flags or bike banners. Or wrapping paper from old newspaper, brown shopping bags or tissue paper. They might like to make plastic bottles. At a summer party, let the kids marker their own tattoos.

But enough. On to the projects. Be sure to read the brief general information on using markers (there's not much to learn) and be sure to read the more specific information about working on various materials, as you need it. I wish you lots of fun and lovely results—and I hope you come to be as fond of markers as I have.

A great deal of thanks and credit go to Mary Lu Guerra, who collaborated with me on this book. Mary Lu designed, executed and illustrated many of the projects.

—LAURA TORBET

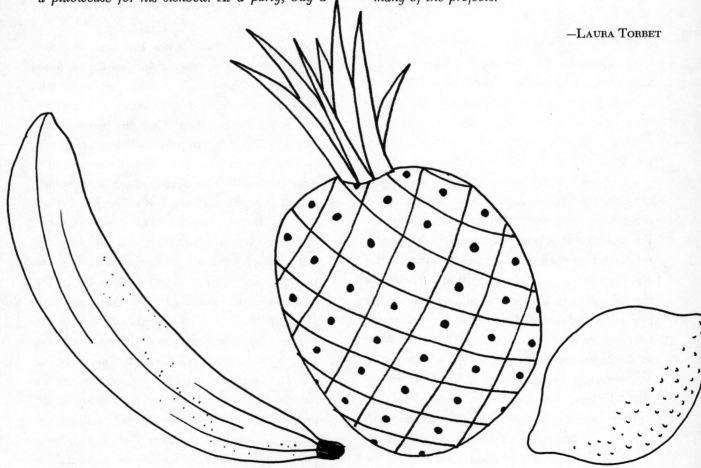

PART 1

General Information

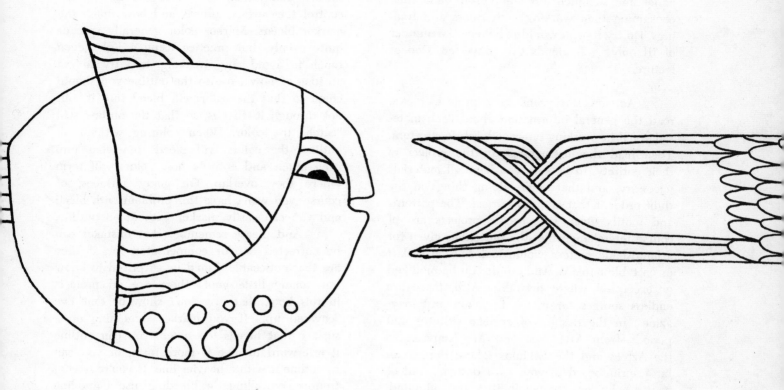

First, a brief (and hopefully inspirational) lecture. For many years and on countless occasions, people who see me working on my various projects who say, "If only I could do that," or "I can't even draw a straight line," or "It must be wonderful to have talent." The truth is that all it takes to do these projects, or anything that doesn't require a highly developed skill, is a little confidence—a little nerve. It's really very hard to mess up a marker project—most small mistakes won't show, and in many cases a mistake can be made to blend in somehow and made to look absolutely normal. Also, many, many of the patterns in this book have been purposely kept simple so that they can be copied freehand, or adapted and changed. There are also illustrations to guide you, many of which can be used as patterns.

Since we're working for the most part with commercially available items, and not something we've made ourselves from scratch, you will often be working with a garment or a piece of furniture of different dimensions and details than the object I've used for the project. Improvising and adapting my ideas somewhat will be necessary, but all the designs are planned so they are easy to adapt. Use the structure and the detailing of *your* marker project to decide which area to color, where to place the various motifs.

I'm a firm believer in drawing freehand—markers lend themselves especially well to a casual line and style. Do try it, or at least try mechanically transferring just the outlines of a motif and doing the rest freehand. I assure you, it's easier than you think, and most surfaces offer some "resistance" to the marker so that you can draw with some control. Another thing that you can do is draw the design very lightly with a pencil, if that is more comfortable for you, and then marker right over the pencil lines—the marker will dissolve the pencil marks. Also, in the case of many woods and fabrics, you have the weave or the grain to guide you in drawing straight lines. It's actually easier and so much less cumbersome and time consuming than working with rulers and tracings. Do try it—you wouldn't believe the number of "If only . . ." friends I've converted. End of lecture.

As you start each new project, please read the general information about each material you'll be working on—wood, fabric, etcetera. Then read the instructions for the project in their entirety, to be sure you have all materials necessary, and that you're doing things in the right order if that is at all critical. The patterns and motifs given for specific projects are of course interchangeable—the butterflies given for a lampshade pattern would look fine on a skirt or on table napkins. And motifs can be modified or excerpted where desirable. Also, there are endless sources for motifs in books and magazines, in the designs of specific cultures and periods—from Art Deco and Art Nouveau to the Aztecs and the Eskimos. These things can be a springboard to your own designs. And of course color scheme possibilities are unlimited, so don't take our color choices literally; use *your* own colors.

In the sections that follow, you'll find information on how to work on specific surfaces, what to do about bleed, what kind of markers and tools you'll need, how to transfer, enlarge and reduce patterns, and how to finish and care for the project with the best results. This information will not be repeated for each project, so be sure and check what you need to know.

Markers and Markering

There's no mystery to using markers—it's just a matter of drawing and coloring. Some surfaces have to be treated with special consideration (markers tend to bleed a bit on wood along the direction of the grain, for example), but there is no special technique to master.

It's helpful to practice a bit with markers, to get the feel of drawing a smooth line, and you should practice on each new type of surface you intend to use to see how much control the surface affords and how much the marker bleeds. Marker color generally spreads quite evenly, but practice using a light, even touch to avoid any streaking, and try to get an idea of how close to the outline you should come so that the color will bleed into it, but not through it—that is, so that the outline will "catch" the color. When coloring without an outline, the colors will bleed somewhat into each other, and entirely new colors will form where they overlap. On many surfaces, of course, you won't have this problem with bleed and you can easily marker without an outline.

And please remember that mistakes can be corrected and/or compensated for, if they are that noticeable. You'd be surprised to know how many little goofs there are on projects in this book that just don't show or that I've "covered up." If you marker something on a surface that bleeds too much, you can outline it afterward to give it more form, or you can re-outline it with a heavier line. If you're having trouble controlling the bleeding, use a fine-line marker, in a color as close to your filler color as possible, to outline the area you're coloring. This will give it a crisp line. You can also use a fine-line marker to color the areas near the edges of a black outline. The fine-line marker dispenses little pigment and is therefore inclined to bleed less than the wide-tip marker. Generally, fine-line markers are used for outlining or drawing, and wide-tip markers for "coloring in."

Also, if you use a color that you don't like, remember that marker color is transparent and you can go over it with another color to lighten, darken or completely change the hue.

Permanent markers are a must for the projects in this book. Most dime stores carry a limited selection of permanent markers, but the widest variety of brands and colors can be found in art supply stores and, to a more limited extent, in craft and hobby shops.

I can't recommend specific brands of markers, but most permanent markers are truly permanent, though I prefer the colors of certain brands and their feel and application. For outlining, I am partial to a type of marker which has a large barrel, but has a pointed tip like a fine-line pen.

Markers *must* be kept covered when not in use, even for a short period of time. Half-dried-up pens are difficult to use and produce streaky color areas. If markers have been left uncapped, they can sometimes be restored to a workable condition by soaking the tips in a glass partially filled with benzene or methyl ethyl ketone. Both are volatile substances, so keep their containers closed and out of reach of children.

A marker whose tip has become blunted or somewhat deformed from overly aggressive use can be sharpened or "shaved" with a razor blade.

Markers, if properly tended, last a long time; if you're planning to use a great deal of one color on a particularly large project, or on a very absorbent surface, be sure to note the color you're using in case you have to replace it. Marker colors seem consistent, so you shouldn't have to worry about a mismatch in the next batch.

Tools and Tips

There are several tools which can be of great help with some of your marker projects.

For drawing straight lines on flat surfaces, use a ruler. If you're working on a circular or curved surface, use a tape measure or a strip of masking tape to guide you.

A T-square is helpful and time saving for quickly ruling parallel straight lines on furniture or three-dimensional objects.

Templates of flexible plastic, with cutouts of various sizes for circles, squares, ovals, etcetera, can be purchased in many dime stores and in art supply stores. These are a great shortcut in drawing repeat motifs and improvising the decorative detailing you'll want on many of your projects.

Sooner or later you'll need a compass to rule accurate circles with markers. There are two solutions to the compass problem. For all but very large circles, you can use a pencil compass, such as you find in most stationery and dime stores. But you'll have to adapt it. To do this, remove the pencil that comes with it, and, using a screwdriver or similar tool, pry open the pencil clamp until it is large enough to accept a marker. Just tape the marker in place. It's a cumbersome solution, but once you've done this, you can interchange whatever markers you may have to use.

For very large circles, you'll have to improvise a compass by tying a string to the marker and looping the other end over the head of a tack at the appropriate distance. Using the tack as the point of the compass, draw your circle, carefully keeping the marker at the full length of the string and maintaining a consistent tautness and pressure.

Transferring Designs

There are many methods of transferring a pattern to your project. The method you use depends on the type of material and surface you're working on.

Direct light method: If you can rig up a light table of some sort, this is one of the easiest methods, since it involves nothing more than tracing. One way is to rig up a light bulb underneath a glass table or a piece of plexiglass or lucite and just trace the pattern through the fabric, paper or whatever. You can also just use light coming through a window by taping your pattern to the window, taping the fabric or paper over the top, and tracing.

Carbon method: Dressmaker's carbon is a simple aid to transferring a pattern. Trace the pattern onto tracing paper. Place a piece of dressmaker's carbon face down in position over the project, place the pattern in position over the carbon and trace over the lines of the pattern with a stylus or ball point pen, pressing firmly. The same effect can be achieved by going over the lines on the back of a pattern with a soft carbon pencil. Place the pattern in position over the project and trace over the lines of the pattern, again with a stylus or ball point pen.

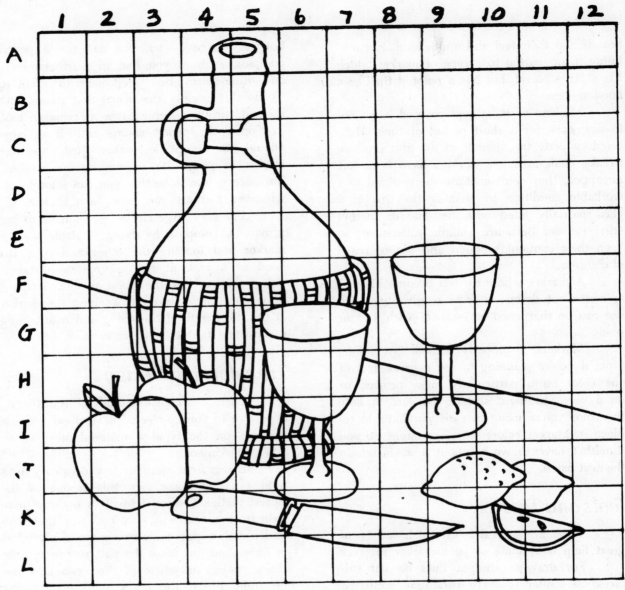

Enlarging and Reducing Designs

If you need to enlarge or reduce a design in this book to fit your project, rule a grid with the same number of squares shown in the illustration, exactly the size that you want your pattern to be. For example, if you're making the pattern three times larger, make each square three times larger. You may want to number the squares along the top and letter the squares along the sides for easy reference. Copy the design directly from the pattern in the book, square by square, to get an accurate reproduction.

Markering on Fabric

Most fabrics take markers beautifully, but various fabrics accept markers differently. Generally, most natural, even-weave fabrics—such as cotton, duck, denim, etcetera—have little tendency to bleed and they absorb the color deeply. Silks and synthetics have a tendency to bleed into the weave of the fabric, and are less absorbent. I like the "bleeding look" and usually try to make it work for me, using softer lines and colors. However, the amount of bleed *can* be controlled by staying further inside the outline of your design and by working quickly and using a light touch with the marker.

When working with fabric, it's a good idea to have a fairly large flat area to use as a work surface. The area should be lightly padded with newspaper or cardboard—both to achieve a good marker line and to catch excess marker color as it bleeds through the fabric. You should also be able to tack or tape the fabric to the work surface to stretch it sufficiently taut and to keep it stationary. Masking tape seems to work best for this purpose.

Fabrics should also be kept flat. Heavy fabric such as denim can usually be worked on as is. Knit T-shirts and some synthetics (which tend to slip around) will need to be stretched and taped to your work surface. If you're working on something which is doubled—such as a skirt or a pillowcase—cardboard or newspaper should be placed between the layers of fabric in the area you are working to prevent the marker from bleeding through to the other side.

Since fabric projects will be washed or cleaned, you should test all marker colors to be sure there isn't a secret "bleeder" in the bunch. There are certain colors, especially in the red-to-pink-to-purple range, that have a tendency to bleed.

Take a small swatch of white fabric, preferably a cotton of some sort, and draw the outline of a square at least one inch long for every color you wish to test. Fill in the squares, one to a color, and indicate next to it the number or name of the color in the square. Then test the swatch as follows:

Press the test swatch with a hot, hot iron. Soak the swatch, laying it out as flat as possible in a small amount of water (enough to comfortably cover the material) and two cups of vinegar for at least fifteen minutes. Then wash it normally in warm water and soap. Check to see if any colors have run outside the black outlines of the squares; if so, eliminate these markers from your fabric "palette." There is no need to retest the colors on each new fabric you use—a bleeder is a bleeder is a bleeder.

The pressing, soaking and washing procedure should be followed the first time you wash any markered project, as the ironing and vinegar soaking help to seal in the color. After this first ordeal, fabrics can be laundered as usual by hand or machine.

Permanent markers will inevitably fade over a period of many washings; if you don't care for the faded look they can be spruced up periodically. Markered fabrics can be dry cleaned, but they will fade considerably in the first cleaning. To give you an idea of the degree of fading to be expected, the swatches shown in the color photo on page 9 were tested as discussed above and they have been machine-washed and dried ten times. Some of the swatches are 100% cotton and others are 100% polyester. Fabric projects that can't be washed —felt hats, chair seats, throw pillows—can be sprayed after markering with Scotchgard or other fabric protector to retard soiling.

Two words of caution: When markering clothing items, avoid markering near the armpits as perspiration causes marker to run. Trying to erase marker from fabric is hopeless, so be a little careful if you want well-defined lines.

Markering on Wood

Wood is one of the most satisfying materials to marker. The marker color goes on as though it were wood stain, but with none of the bother and with so many more colors to choose from. The wood absorbs the color beautifully, yet the grain of the wood still shows through.

Wood can be worked on raw, or it can be stained first if you prefer a darker color. Do remember that the darker you stain the wood, the less the marker color will show up. If you have a piece of wood furniture that has become scarred or soiled, markers can rejuvenate it quite well. If it is stained a very dark color already, you can scrape the finish down a bit, or you may just want to paint it (flat or enamel paint will do) and marker on the painted surface.

On soft woods, marker color will tend to bleed along the grain. The bleed can be controlled by working carefully. If the wood bleeds too much or if your design is too detailed to control the bleed, it can be checked by sealing the wood with plastic, varnish or shellac. My experience has been that spray products work best—they're easy to apply, they're fast-drying, and they go on in a thin, even coat. Plastic or polyurethane sprays seem to work best, since the ingredients don't seem to conflict in any way with the markers. A sealer coat will prevent the marker from bleeding, but it will also prevent the wood from absorbing too much of the marker, and thus cut down on the intensity of the color.

Personally, I prefer to deal with the bleeding problem by working very carefully, rather than by sealing the wood. And if you're very careful, you can scrape off the excess with the flat of a razor blade or mat knife, that is, tilt the blade or knife a little and scrape off unwanted color. After color has been applied, however, I always seal the finished work with a coat of a plastic-base spray, to protect the wood and to keep the marker from water damage and soil. A couple of light coats work best. Brush-on products such as varnish or shellac are chancy as they tend to darken the surface, and if applied too quickly they can dissolve some of the marker color.

Incidentally, wood that has been chipped, stained or discolored can often be easily repaired by markering with a color to match the original wood finish. Since markers are widely used by designers and architects, the marker companies make colors which correspond to most types of wood.

Markering on Leather and Suede

Leather and suede are ideal surfaces to marker. They take markers as if they were made for each other. Then too, markers are much easier to use and cheaper than leather dyes, and they come in a much wider range of colors.

Old, worn leather and suede garments, purses, belts, shoes, etcetera, can be beautifully rejuvenated with markers and given a whole new life. If you just want to restore a scuffed shoe or a worn purse, you can color the area with a marker that matches the worn leather, usually rather successfully. On something more complicated, be a little careful as you can't erase marker from leather and suede.

There are no special tricks. Draw just as you would on paper; you will notice that suede absorbs quite a bit of color. Test the markers on an area of the leather or suede that won't be seen to see how much the colors darken.

Suede takes marker perfectly. I recommend, however, that you spray the finished project with a silicone spray or any product recommended for protecting and waterproofing suede. To finish smooth leathers, you can use the standard products recommended for suede and leather, or even a plastic spray such as Varathane.

To give a real leather quality to the bright marker colors, I usually use a bit of antique leather finish such as Feibing's which is sold in many craft stores. A small jar of a light to medium color, such as tan, costs well under a dollar and can be used for several projects.

The antique is very easy to apply. Put a generous amount on a rag, enough to cover the entire project or an entire area with one application. Quickly apply the antique over the entire surface, being sure to coat all edges, etcetera. Then, take another rag and wipe off any excess, as the color will darken quickly if it's left on. You'll find that you can simulate various grains and textures by controlling the direction and motion of the cloth. The amount of antique you use and the time you leave it on will control the depth of the color. After removing the excess, buff and polish the leather with another dry rag or a shoe brush.

Markering on Glass

Markering on glass is very easy, and looks lovely. Here are a couple of pointers. Glass absorbs no color, so only a light film of color will adhere to the surface. Therefore, strong, bright colors are called for. Pale shades won't show up. Strong colors are especially important when markering windows or light bulbs where light coming through will tend to dilute the color still more.

A streaky marker quality on glass is inevitable, but it looks okay. Because glass is so slippery, you will not have a great deal of control over the marker line, unless you're very steady. If you've really goofed, try scraping it off with the flat of a razor blade or mat knife, that is, tilt it only a little. Or try removing it with a solvent such as methyl ethyl ketone or one with a benzene base. Of course the best way is to keep your motifs loose and simple so you won't have this problem.

Finally, marker will not stick to glass permanently unless it is sprayed; a plastic spray such as Varathane works well. It should be sprayed in a light, even coat to leave a minimal film on the glass. Any areas which must remain clear (for example, the mirror on page 11) should be masked while spraying.

Markering on Plastic

The results of markering plastics can be varied, as they depend on the type of plastic and its surface finish. It is therefore difficult to give any steadfast advice about markering it. The solvent in markers "attacks" the surface of many plastics, etching color into the material. On other plastics the marker might just skim across the surface with a streakiness or little intensity of color.

Therefore to really know how your particular plastic will react to marker, the best test is to marker it in an unobtrusive spot. Here you should be able to discover the degree of control you can exercise over the marker and the quality of the colors (whether it streaks, for example). You can also find out whether the surface will take the marker by nicking it with your thumbnail to see if it flakes. This is especially important before embarking on a massive project, only to discover there is no way to prevent your handiwork from chipping off. Unlike wooden projects plastic ones cannot be sprayed to protect them, as the spray lightly lifts the surface of the plastic and your design is liable to slide off your object onto the floor.

The plastics that you are dissolving as you work can often clog the felt tip of the marker. If after you start working on a plastic project you notice that the colors seem to be drying too rapidly, stop drawing on the plastic and scribble with the marker on a scrap of paper or a rag until the colors are freed and begin to flow again. If the size of the project warrants the investment of the labor, you might try tacking a piece of hopsacking or sailcloth near the surface you will be working on for a really convenient place to clean the marker. Dipping the marker in solvent will also release the plastic from the tip.

If you've made a mistake and you can't really cover it up, try scraping it off very gently with the flat of a razor blade or mat knife, that is, tilt the blade a little and scrape off the marker.

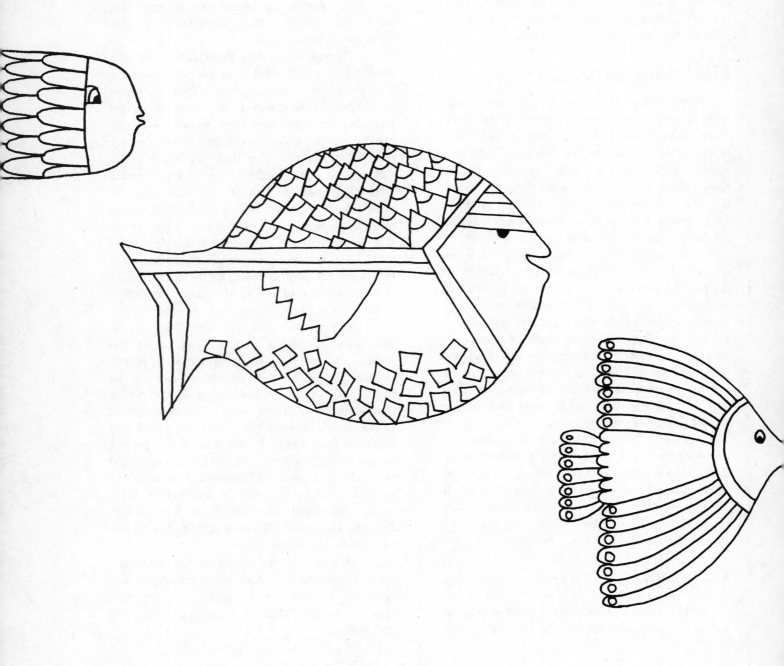

PART 2

You Can Do Anything
with Markers

Each square equals 2″

TABLE TOP

TABLE SIDE

Parson's Table

An unfinished wood Parson's table is fun and easy to decorate with a colorful geometric design. The one shown is 24"L x 24"W x 24"H (60 x 60 x 60 cm.), but any size will adapt to the same design.

Rule the entire table into 2" (5 cm.) squares lightly with a pencil. This is the easiest way. Later you can erase the extra lines. Do the top of the table first. If your table-top is an odd length (not an even multiple of two inches), mark your rules from the outside of the table toward the center, leaving the odd amount of space in the center.

Rule the sides of the table as shown in the illustration. There are two rows of four squares on each side.

The legs on this table are 2½" (6.75 cm.) wide and, as seen in the pattern, each side of the leg has four 2" squares and four ½" (1.25 cm.) rectangles, measuring from the bottom of the leg. Follow the illustration to make sure that the 2" squares fall in the same place on each leg (the outside corner).

Rule the design for the center of the table-top as shown. Erase all extraneous pencil lines.

Using a straightedge or ruler, draw in the lines with a black fine-line marker.

Choose and plan a color scheme and carefully color in the squares, making sure each corner of the table-top, each side and each leg are colored to match. I tried a sort of rainbow effect, working from yellow on the corners in to greens, blues, and warm reds and pinks in the center.

Spray the completed table with several coats of polyurethane finish.

Shown in color on page 9

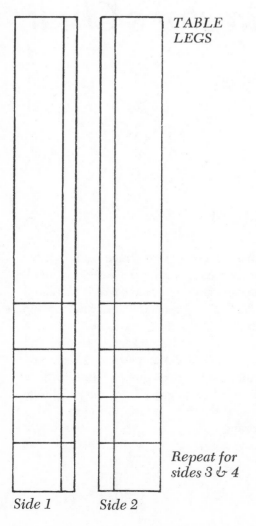

TABLE LEGS

Repeat for sides 3 & 4

Side 1   Side 2

Shown in color on page 11

Director's Director's Chair

Replaceable director's chair seats come in a wide range of colors suitable for markering. Or perhaps a chair that you have already would be grateful for a marker design to disguise wear and soil. These covers can be easily removed for laundering. It's very important to test your colors for permanency, so that they don't come off the chair seat onto yours.

The chair here has a camera on the seat and a simulated film strip across the back.

Stretch the seat cover tautly over a work surface and tape or pushpin it in place. Then enlarge the camera design, trace and transfer it onto the seat cover, using the carbon method.

The camera design on the seat is markered in black only. For the chair back, rule the top and bottom borders first with the sprocket design. A section of this border is shown, full size, so you can trace the pattern. Then draw in the "frames" of the picture. I chose to do a sunrise in various stages—it's a simple design and you can see the "action" progress. Also, the big orange sun looks good on the bright yellow canvas.

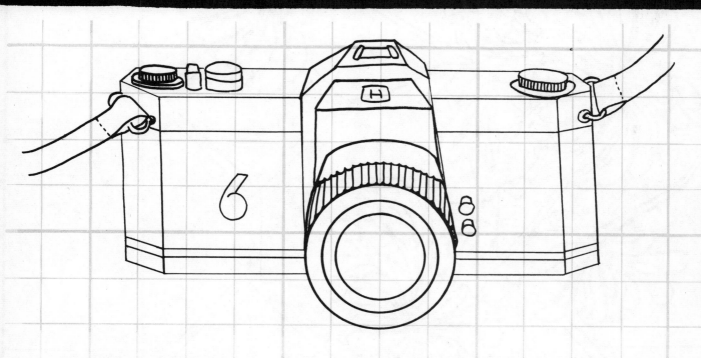

TOP

Flowered Director's Chair

Shown in color on page 13

Chrysanthemums were combined with a windowpane motif to integrate the director's chair into a living room where these two motifs were repeated on a rug and curtains.

Stretch the seat cover tautly over a work surface and tape or pushpin it in place. You may find that it is okay to work on it in place on the chair, especially if it is a new seat cover and fits snugly. Pencil in the flower motif, or look around you in your own room and notice any single design on your slipcovers or wallpaper, for instance, that you could easily trace and transfer onto the seat cover. You can color it immediately or wait until the design is completed to be sure your composition pleases you.

Next, rule in the large windowpane squares. The squares measure 4¼″ (11.25 cm.) and the border lines are ⅜″ (9 mm.) thick. Here again you can draw in a background that may be used in the decor of the room such as stripes, plaids or polka dots. The smaller intersecting squares measure 2″ (5 cm.) and I found it simpler to cut a 2″ square template from a sturdy piece of cardboard and trace it in. You can, of course, enlarge the pattern and trace and transfer it all together onto the seat cover.

The flowers were colored with a combination of reds for the petals and outlined in reddish brown. The leaves were colored in green with streaks of the same color blue that was used for the smaller squares. Last of all, the bars of the windowpane were filled in with black, using the ruler to achieve a crisp line.

You can use this technique to make your own designs. It is so nice to complete a room by unifying it with your own hand, and often it is hard to find the right print or the right color fabric that turns the trick. So with marker in hand, create it!

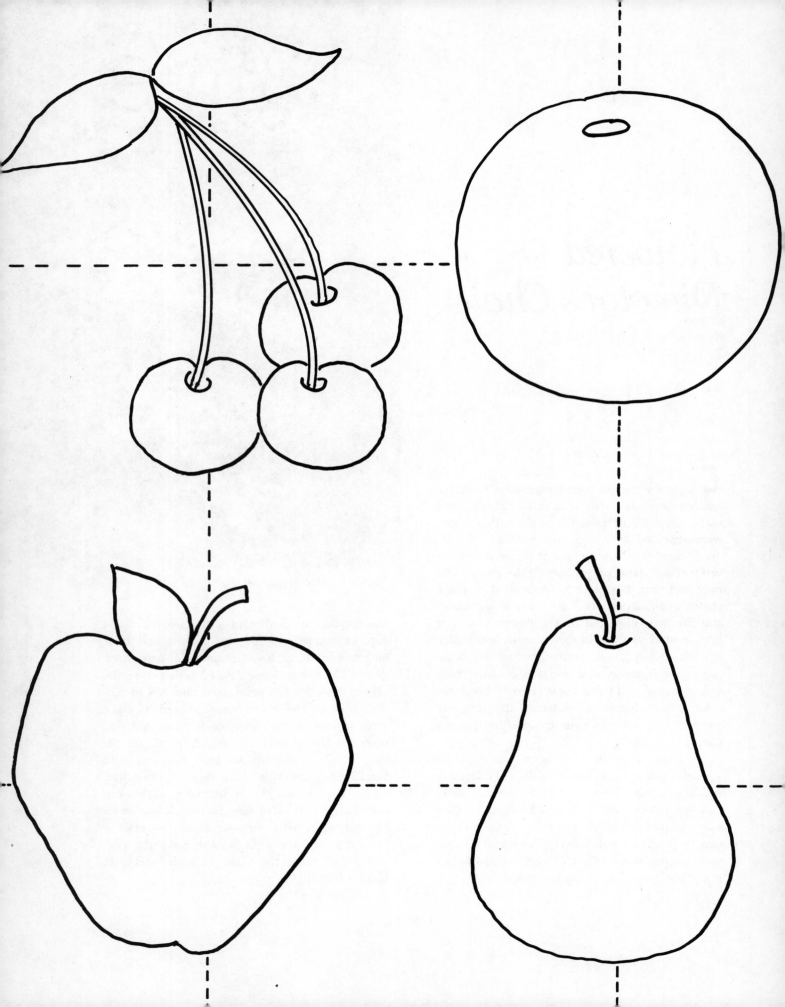

Chest of Drawers

With its rustic country charm, this chest of drawers would look nice anywhere in your house. The dimensions of this chest are 34″H x 21″L x 13″W (85 x 52.5 x 32.5 cm.).

We markered directly on the raw wood, but you might want to lightly stain your chest first, especially if the raw wood is very pale. Don't feel you have to follow our pattern; arrange the fruit as it looks best on your piece of furniture.

Four stencils are all that is needed to do the job. Stencils are easy to make and can be re-used and adapted to other projects as well. These fruit stencils might be used on curtains or table napkins in the same room as the chest.

The best papers for cutting stencils are oaktag or a heavy waxy paper sold in art supply stores specifically for stencilling. Light-weight, not-too-crumbly cardboard will also do the job. Stencils should be cut with a large mat knife or X-acto knife. You don't have to cut separate stencils for each color; you'll be able to separate the colors enough by working carefully with the markers.

Transfer the designs to the stencil paper by the carbon method and cut the stencils. As you can see, there is a drawer each of apples, pears, oranges, and cherries, with the design continuing around the sides of the chest, and two rows of fruit on the top. Mark a pencil line for the horizontal center of each drawer, and for the vertical center of each piece of fruit, as shown in the pattern. Lay the stencils in place on the chest, matching up these pencil marks with those on the stencils. Color in the fruit, using wide-tip markers. If the markers tend to bleed under the stencils, work quickly, and move the marker from the stencil in toward

Shown in color on page 10

the area being colored. When you're through, erase any pencil lines that show. For finishing touches, color in any knobs, feet or other decorative trim on the chest.

You might, if you wish, make a stencil from any of a number of simple motifs in this book, and do a repeat motif design in the same manner as the fruit.

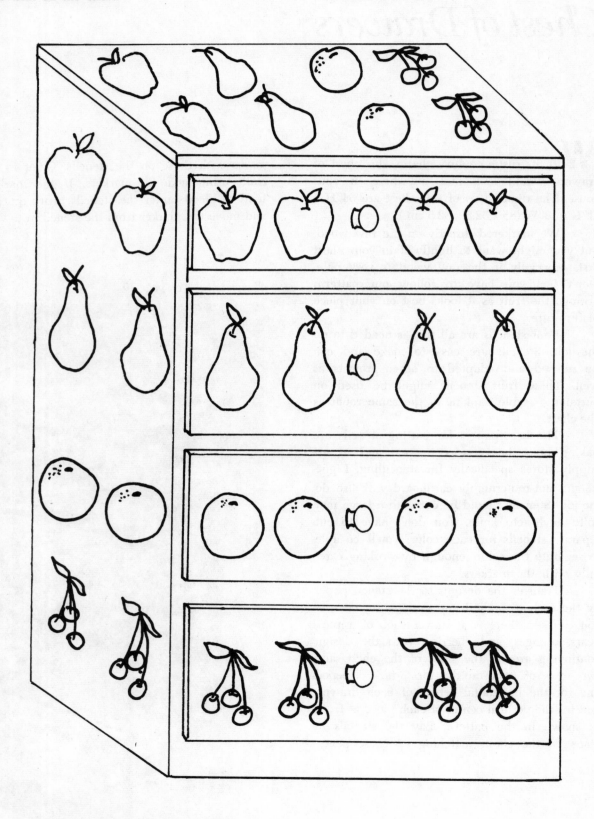

Shown in color on page 12

End Tables

These triangular end tables can be used separately or, when pushed together, double as a chessboard or a checkerboard. It's not necessary to have two tables; the same design would work fine on a square table or storage cube. The motif is a perfect example of stealing from other sources—in this case, directly from the design of the Oriental rug in the room where they were used. We also copied the colors from the Oriental rug—maroons, pinks, ochre, dark green and blue.

Here are the measurements of these tables (when pushed together): 32″W x 32″L x 23″H (80 x 80 x 57.5 cm.). To begin the design, find the center of the table and mark off the entire top in pencil into 2″ (5 cm.) squares, going from the center out to the sides. This is to be sure that the chess/checkerboard is centered and that any odd measurements (less or more than 2″) are left around the edges. It also provides a guide to drawing the rest of the design. Any extra lines can be erased later.

If you have a T-square, make use of it here. You can rule the squares very easily just by running the square along the edges of the table to get a right angle. Now follow the illustration for the diagonal lines and the semicircles. You may, however, want to enlarge the design for the flower in each corner and make a tracing-paper pattern. To start the sides, determine the bottom center of the side and mark it, again with the tables pushed together. Rule a line from this point to the line connecting the inside band of the row of stripes on the top. (See Illustration.) After the design is pencilled in, go over everything with a black marker. I used a fine-line marker, so that the black line pretty much disappeared during the coloring process.

TABLE SIDE

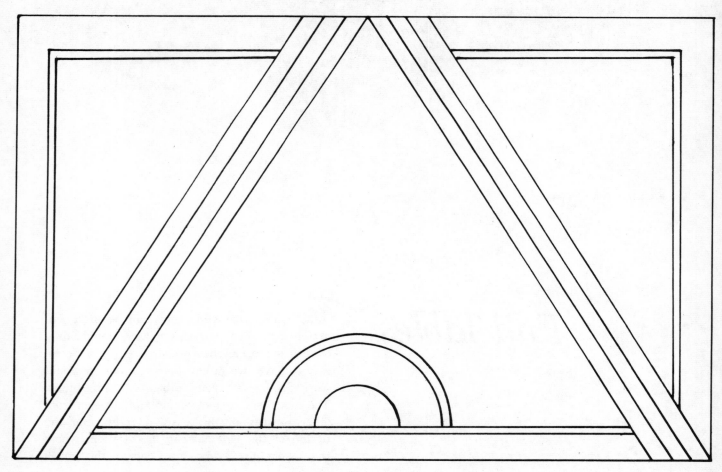

Complete inside square lines first

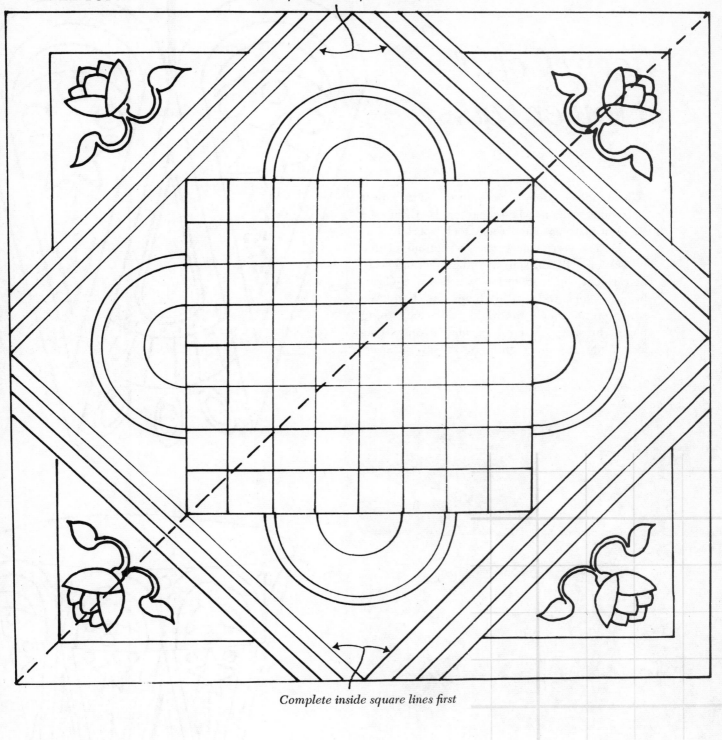

Complete inside square lines first

Terra Cotta Flower Pots

Common garden variety terra cotta flower pots look super when markered. Even the simplest designs make them look special.

Test your colors on the bottom of the pot—color will darken considerably and very pale colors will tend to look washed out. Clear, bright colors and earthy tones are best. We stuck pretty much to bright reds and strong pinks, browns, clear blues and greens. Pots look quite nice in a grouping of several sizes,

Shown in color on page 12

[42]

and the patterns given here will adapt to most sizes. However, in some cases you may have to enlarge or reduce the design or adapt the pattern to fit your pot, adding or subtracting some of the design elements as needed.

With the geometric designs, you have to account for the angle of the pot in drawing straight vertical lines. Use a tape measure to guide you in making straight lines around the circular circumference and also for vertical lines.

For patterns like the cactus pot and the one with all the buildings, transfer the designs using the carbon method. You'll have to improvise a bit where the patterns meet. A group of pots of varying sizes done with the same design motif, such as the cactuses, would look very well together.

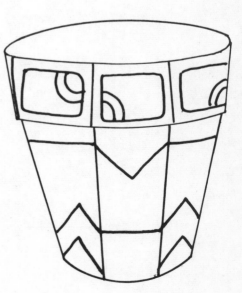

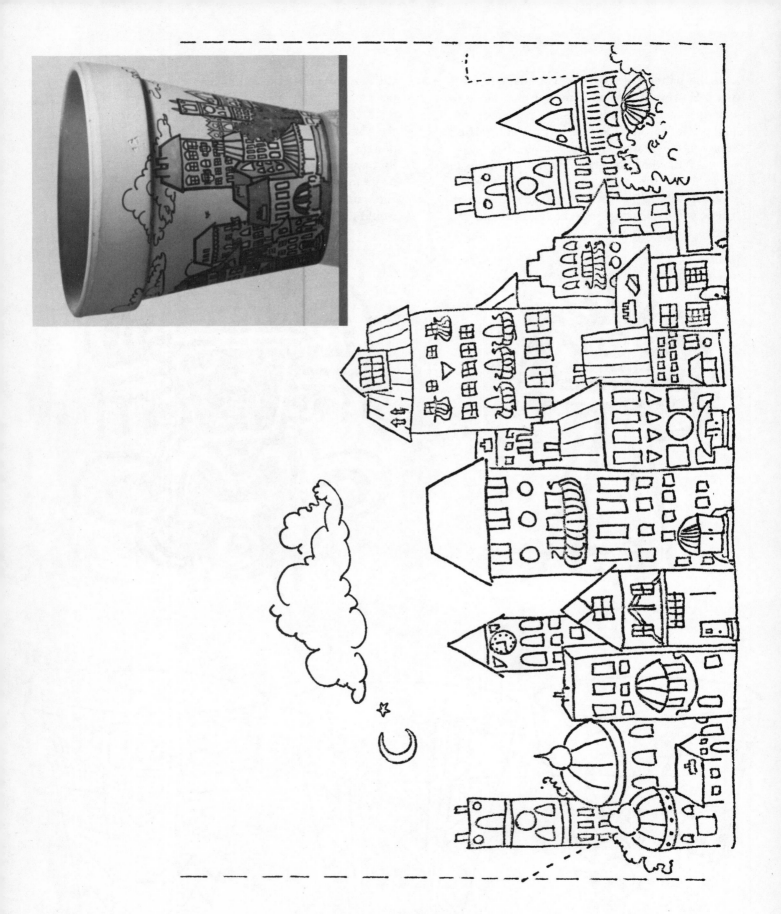

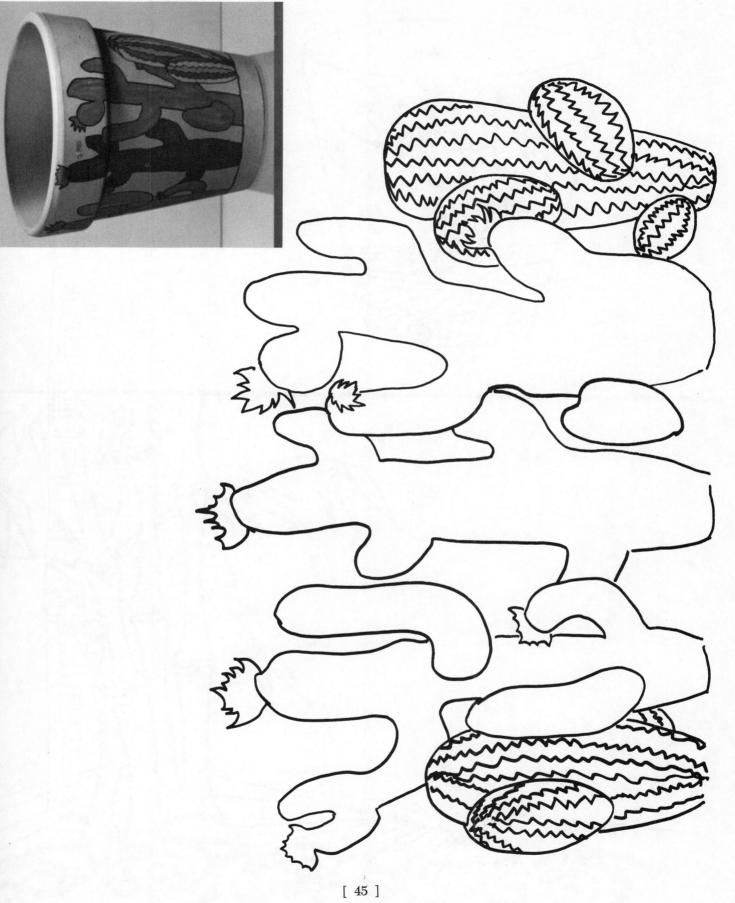

Plastic Flower Pot

The Japanese motif on this plastic flower pot is easy to do, repeating several simple motifs all around. It's the perfect home for a spidery plant in a sunny window.

The pot we used is 10″ (25 cm.) high, but the design will adapt easily to almost any size. First, draw the scrolly water all around the bottom of the pot. It's a bit difficult to follow an exact pattern when working on this slick, curved surface, so the easiest way to do

it is freehand. Then, make a carbon pattern for the bamboo tree, and transfer the tree pattern at intervals around the pot. Do the straight lines, connecting the trees and the water last.

For color, we used serene blues and greens. You'll find that on plastic your colors will have to be darker than usual because the smooth surface will not absorb any of the pigment.

Shown in color on page 13

TOP

This motif is repeated on each section

Shown in color on page 9

Window Box

This small wooden crate became a charming window box with a coat of paint and a geometric marker design. Many containers which you might ordinarily discard can be put to new uses. If the surface is not receptive to marker or if it is too dark, you can give it a coat of spray paint for a more suitable base.

You'll notice several projects throughout this book that have a checkerboard motif. That's because they were all designed for use in the same room and the checkerboard is the unifying feature.

The box shown here is approximately 6"H x 10"L x 5"W (15 x 25 x 12.5 cm.) and is markered predominantly in a stark red-and-black combination. Enlarge the pattern to the size you need and then transfer the design by the carbon method. If your box is a different shape, you can always adapt this design by adding or subtracting the motif as needed. And by all means experiment with color.

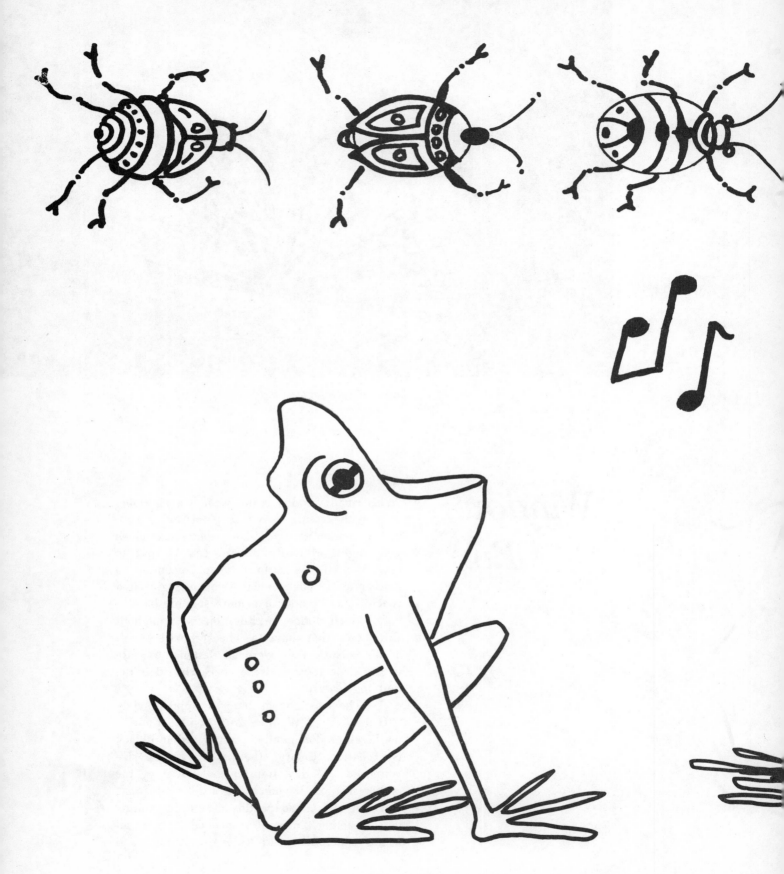

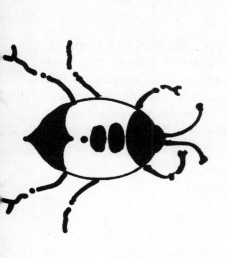

Shown in color on page 9

Watering Cans

Your watering can may become a decorative part of your home if you marker it prettily. The plastic of these watering cans takes marker very well; the surface even seems to absorb some of the color, making it very permanent and waterproof.

Because you're dealing with a curved surface, small motifs and simple patterns are the easiest to do. Patterns are given for the frogs and bugs on this watering can. Trace and transfer them. The design and structure of the raised lines on this particular can determined their position. The design of your watering can will help you place the motifs where they look best.

The bright yellow plastic looks rather

sprightly with the green singing frog and brightly colored bugs of every description.

The checkerboard pattern on this watering can follows raised lines in the plastic, so there was no need to measure and rule lines. You can, of course, adapt this design to your watering can. Do the spider and web freehand, or, if you like, enlarge the pattern, trace and transfer it. We just used black marker on this white plastic watering can but you can use any color you like. Stick to one or two colors so that the design will show up.

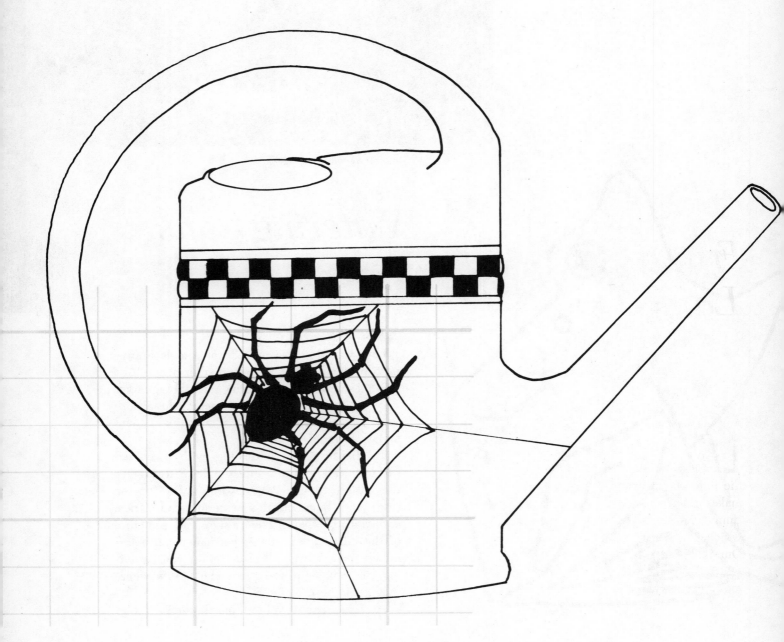

Fruit Tree Lampshade

Shown in color on page 13

Lampshades are perfect for markers because the light coming through the transparent colors makes them appear extra brilliant. Here is a sunny, almost tropical-looking lampshade on which the design motif is repeated four times. Our lampshade, a dime-store purchase, is 10¼″ (25.5 cm.) high. It is made of a stiff, woven-look material and does not give nor does it bleed as much as silk or synthetic lampshades.

When markering a circular project, especially one with a repeat motif, a small amount of pre-planning will assure a balanced arrangement of your concept.

Measure the top circumference of your shade. Using tracing paper, enlarge (or reduce) the pattern given here so that the width of the design at the top is a quarter of the circumference of the top of your shade. Any adjustment in the height of the pattern, if needed, can be most easily accomplished by lengthening or shortening the "tree trunks." When planning the height of your design, take into account that the rims of some lampshades will not transmit much light.

Darken the lines of your tracing-paper pattern with a black marker.

Now you must mark off the shade in four equal sections. Place the measuring tape around the top circumference of the shade, and make light pencil marks to divide it in

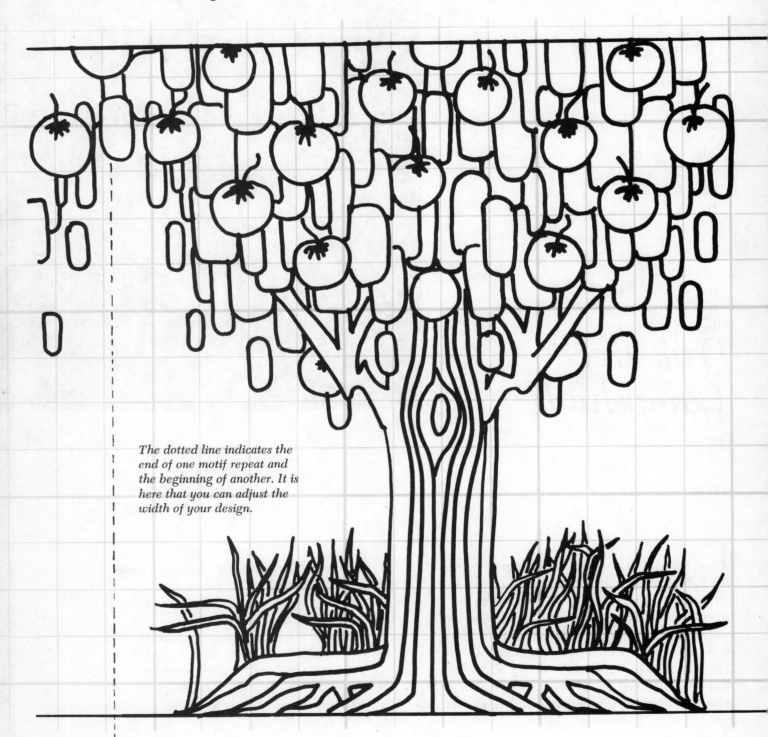

The dotted line indicates the end of one motif repeat and the beginning of another. It is here that you can adjust the width of your design.

quarters. Make a light pencil mark at the bottom of the shade directly below one of the marks at the top. Using this first mark as your guide, run the tape measure around the bottom circumference, and again mark it off in quarters.

(To facilitate markering straight horizontal lines on a round shape, a rubber band, ribbon, string or tape is useful as a guide. A weighted string, hung from the top rim of the shade, will give you an accurate perpendicular line.)

Now, line up your tracing-paper pattern with one of the sections on the shade, placing the pattern *inside the shade*. Use the marks you've made at the top and bottom of the shade as your guide, and tape the pattern in place with masking tape. Attach the shade to a lamp base, turn on the light, and lightly pencil-trace the design onto the shade. Remove the paper pattern, retape and trace the design on the *opposite* section (not the adjoining one); it will be easy to adjust the two side sections if there is any overlap. Finally, retape and trace the two side sections. It's on these two sections that you will have to make the designs "fit," by making any little adjustments necessary to make the motifs come together smoothly.

Draw the outlines of the design with a dark fine-line marker. You may find it easier to work with the lampshade on your lap rather than on a table.

Color! We used oranges, yellows and greens, but you may prefer apples in your trees and a blue sky. Coloring your tracing-paper pattern and holding it up to the light will give you some indication of how your color scheme will look; however, this is only an indication, as the marker colors will appear somewhat lighter on the tracing paper.

Protect the finished lampshade by spraying it with a coat of Scotchgard or other soil retardant.

[55]

Peacock Lampshade

Peacocks are another of nature's more colorful creations. The black outlining and background on this lampshade really sets off the bright colors which bleed together nicely, just like on a real-life peacock.

This shade is 13″ (32.5 cm.) high, and like the butterfly shade (page 58), it is divided into eight sections. If the wire framework of

Shown in color on page 11

Side panel

the shade divides your lampshade into eight sections, use the struts as your guiding lines. If not, mark off the sections by the method described in Fruit Tree Lampshade (page 55). (You will, of course, have to divide each of the quarters in half here.)

The peacock is centered on three sections, with its body in the middle of the center section. A second peacock (exactly the same) is placed directly opposite, on the other side of the shade. The peacock feather motif is used on the two side panels between the peacocks. Make a tracing-paper pattern the size you need (enlarging or reducing as required), and transfer it to the shade according to the method described in Fruit Tree Lampshade (page 55).

To get the best effect, color the peacock feathers in clear, bright shades of pink, magenta, purple, blue, yellow and orange, overlapping the colors a bit where they come together to create entirely new hues. To protect your shade, spray with Scotchgard or some other soil retardant.

*Shade is black
from this line
out to nearest strut and top and bottom*

Shown in color on page 12

Butterfly Lampshade

Here is a particularly appealing lampshade with butterflies as the motif. We colored two of the butterflies in very strong colors, and the two on the other side in soft pastel shades. The effect is quite different.

Silk or synthetic lampshades are ideal because the colors come out very intense, and the material is easy to draw on. Then too, the colors bleed, and you can get lovely effects where the light comes through the overlapping areas.

The lampshade we used is 11″ (27.5 cm.) high and was divided into eight sections by the wire framework of the shade. There are four butterflies with their bodies centered vertically over every other wire strut, so the lampshade itself provided the structure for laying out the design. If your lampshade doesn't have this wire framework, mark off the sections by the method described in Fruit Tree Lampshade (page 55). (You will, of course, have to divide each of the quarters in half here.)

There are two butterflies which alternate around the shade. Make a tracing-paper pattern the size you need (enlarging or reducing as required), and transfer it to the shade according to the method described for the Fruit Tree Lampshade (see page 55). When placing the tracing-paper pattern inside the shade be sure to center the body of the butterfly along the wire strut.

Go over your pencil tracings with a black fine-line marker, then use your imagination with the coloring—butterflies come in more colors than markers!

To protect the finished lampshade, spray it with a coat of Scotchgard or other soil retardant.

Shown in color on page 13

Cigar Box

Unpainted wooden boxes are available in most hobby and craft stores, in many shapes and sizes. This one, 8½" x 10" (21.25 x 25 cm.), is perfect for a cigar box. Other standard sizes make good jewelry boxes, sewing kits, recipe holders, or whatever. Markered boxes make fine gifts, because you can personalize them and marker them with a motif appropriate to the interests or hobbies of the person you're giving it to. This one I monogrammed for my father as a birthday gift. You'll find several alphabet patterns on pages 194-200 which you can use to copy or trace monograms and messages onto your projects.

This pattern has 10 cigars, ⅞" x 7⅜" (2.25 x 18.5 cm.). I found that the marker bled somewhat along the horizontal grain of the wood, so I did all the small areas with fine-line markers and used the shading technique shown in the illustration. Also, all around the edges of the cigars on the top of the box, I used a dark red to cover and compensate for the bleed.

Enlarge the pattern to the size you need, trace and transfer it. (If the box you're using is a different size, you can add or subtract cigars as needed, or shorten or lengthen the cigars in the pattern.) The sides of the box are ruled in horizontal stripes of random width. To rule these lines, decide on the width of the stripes, and make a mark for the appropriate distances at each corner. Use a ruler to connect the marks with a black fine-line marker.

The monogram can be placed anywhere on the box—this one is tilted and off-center on the top of the box. Place the outlines of the monogram motif wherever it seems right to you, and trace your monogram letters from one of the alphabets. I went over the top, bottom, and sides of each of the cigars again with the same color I'd used for the first coat, to give them a shaded, more dimensional look.

No preliminary staining was needed for this box as the wood was quite dark to begin with. If the box you're using is very pale, you may want to stain it first.

The finished box can be given a coat of polyurethane spray, shellac or other finish to give it luster and durability. And, if you like, you can marker the inside of the box or line it with fabric or paper.

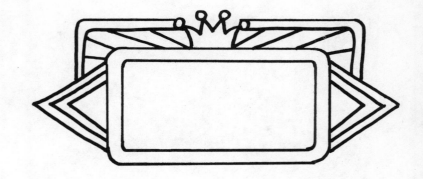

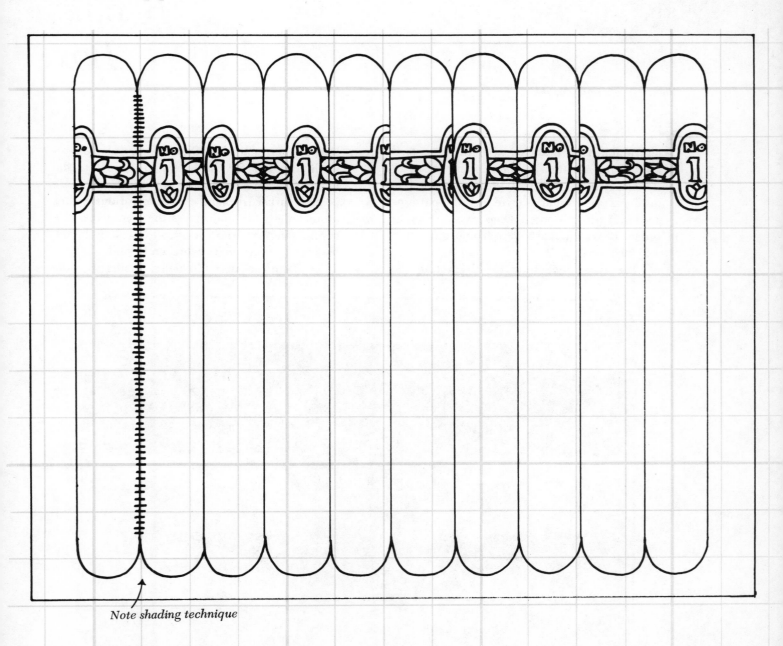

Note shading technique

Recipe Box

Shown in color on page 11

This unfinished wood box holds standard 3″ x 5″ (7.5 x 12.5 cm.) file cards and seems to be a stock item in most craft stores. If your box is a different size, enlarge or reduce the patterns as needed. I use this one to keep favorite recipes in order. It would make a welcome gift for a friend who cooks.

The basic technique for decorating the box is very simple. Choose several pale-to-medium colors for the background, so that the black silhouettes will show up well. Using these colors, marker freehand stripes of various widths around the sides and across the top of the box, overlapping the colors a bit, so that they blend. We used aqua, pink, ochre and coral.

Transfer the silhouette motifs by the

carbon method. The spoon-and-fork design goes on the front side of the box, the "FOOD" on top, the cup and saucer on the back, the jug and the shaker on either side. You can, of course, switch them around, adjusting the design as required. Draw the outline of each design with a black fine-line marker for minimal bleed, and fill in with a black wide-tip marker.

Many other sizes are available in unfinished wood boxes. Some are ideal for jewelry, sewing, stationery, and buttons. You can do your own design on these boxes, using the above method.

Lap Desk

Shown in color on page 12

This unfinished wood lap desk seems to be a standard item in many craft and hobby stores. With an appropriate design, it would make an attractive gift for almost anyone. The dimensions of this desk are 10″L x 14″W x 4½″H (25 x 35 x 11.25 cm.).

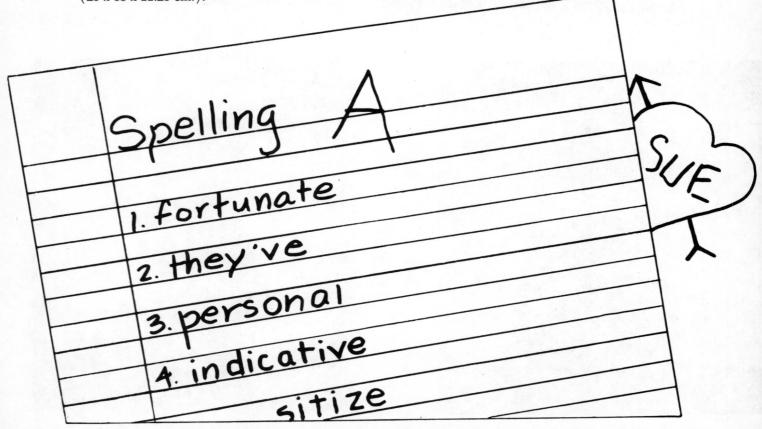

The elements of the design—pencil sharpener, eraser, inkwell, pen and pencil slot, spelling paper, etcetera, are all positioned in the photo, but you can shift them around as you wish to adapt them to the size of your project. The large pencil on the front of the desk can easily be shortened or lengthened to fit whatever you're working on.

Enlarge the patterns where necessary and transfer the design by the carbon method. Test your colors on the bottom of the box to be sure you're getting the unique yellow of the pencil and the paper, and the pink of the eraser. (Remember that the wood will darken the color.) Use brown markers to give the desk a fake wood grain and texture. Use a dark brown fine-line marker to "carve" the heart and initials into the desk.

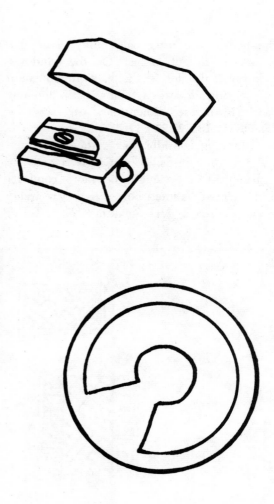

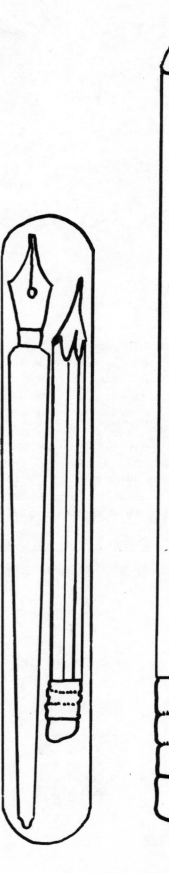

*Shown in color
on page 11*

Birdhouse

This birdhouse originally came in the form of an unfinished wood box at my local hobby shop. Now my city birds will live in country cottage splendor. Patterns are given for each side of the box and for the roof; they can easily be transferred to the box using the carbon method. The simplest way to do the roof is to first go over the entire surface with the color you choose before putting in any detailing.

On the sides of the box, transfer the pattern first. Then fill in the background color of the house (we used pale blue). Save the fake "beams" to put in last. On the windows and shutters, also fill in the background color before putting in any detailing with fine-line markers. Birdhouse dimensions are 5¼"W x 8½"L x 6½"H (13 x 21.25 x 17.25 cm.).

You may consider this cottage too provincial for your birds. If you have ravens in your backyard, they might be more comfortable in a classic haunted house. If they're trend conscious, perhaps a colonial manse . . .

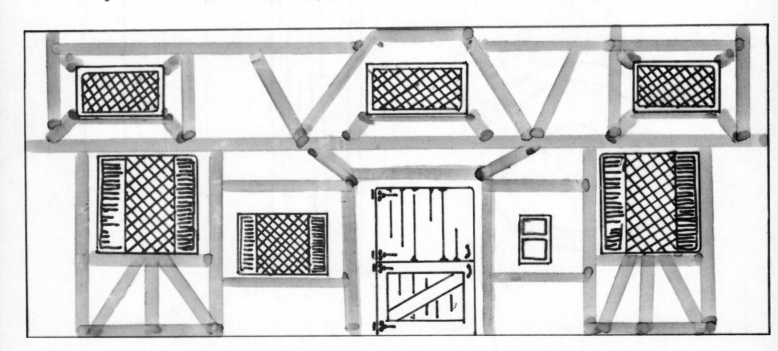

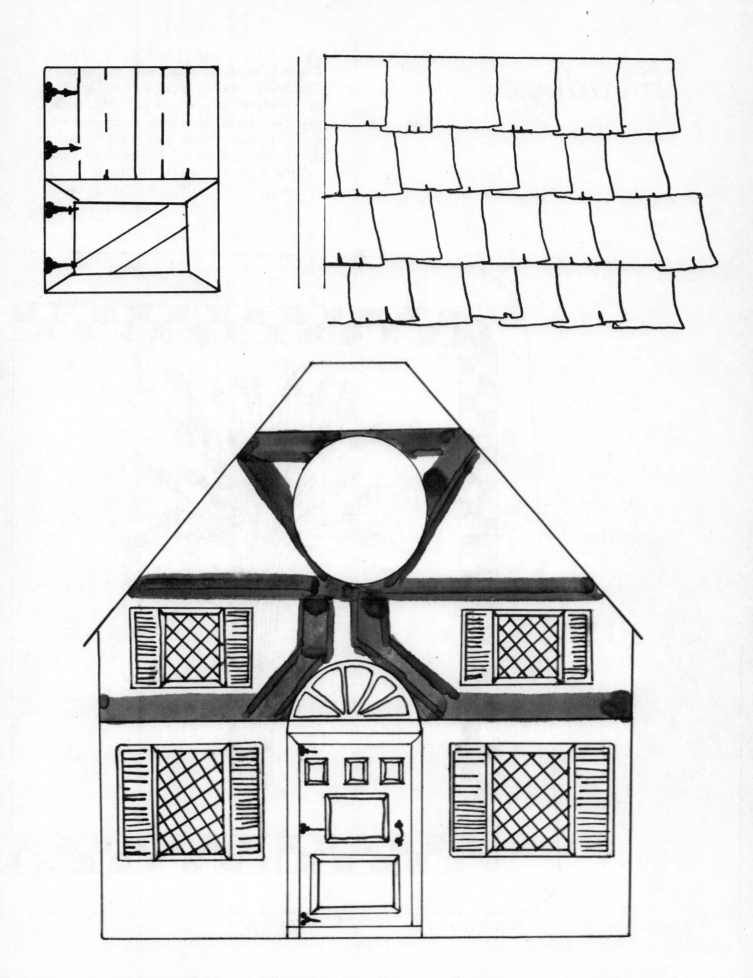

Breadbox

A sheaf of wheat, traditionally the symbol of abundance, seemed an appropriate motif for this breadbox. The box, an old 1940s vintage, was sprayed with white enamel before starting work. The raised metal patterning on the box served as a guide for placing the checkerboard and the individual motifs. The block lettering style is in keeping with the style of the box.

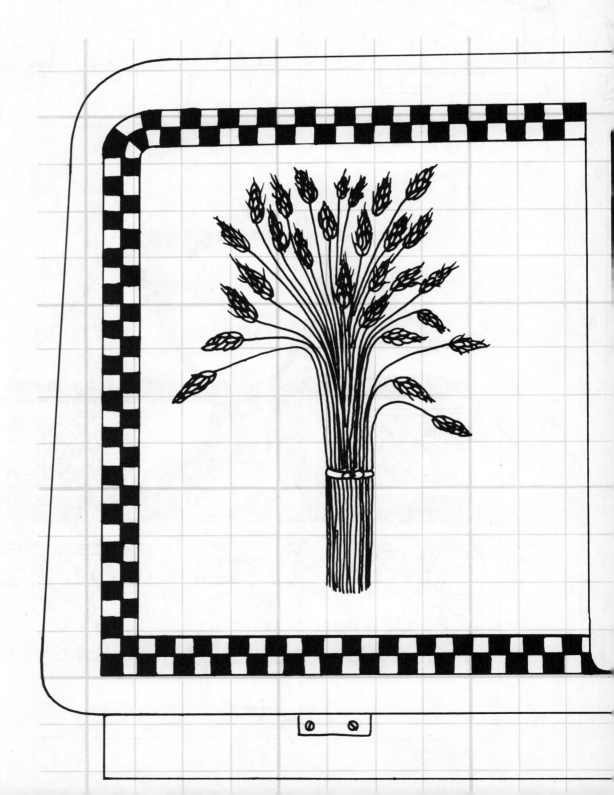

This breadbox is approximately 9″W x 16″L x 9½″H (22.5 x 40 x 23.75 cm.).

Positioning the elements in this pattern will depend on the size and shape of the box you are markering. Elements such as the checkerboard pattern and the diagonal stripes should go where they fit and where they look best. You can make a tracing-paper pattern (en-larging to the size you need) for the sheaf of wheat and the word "BREAD" and transfer them. Our breadbox was done in black marker only, but it might also look nice with the checkerboard in red, and a golden sheaf of wheat.

Seal the finished project with a coat of polyurethane spray.

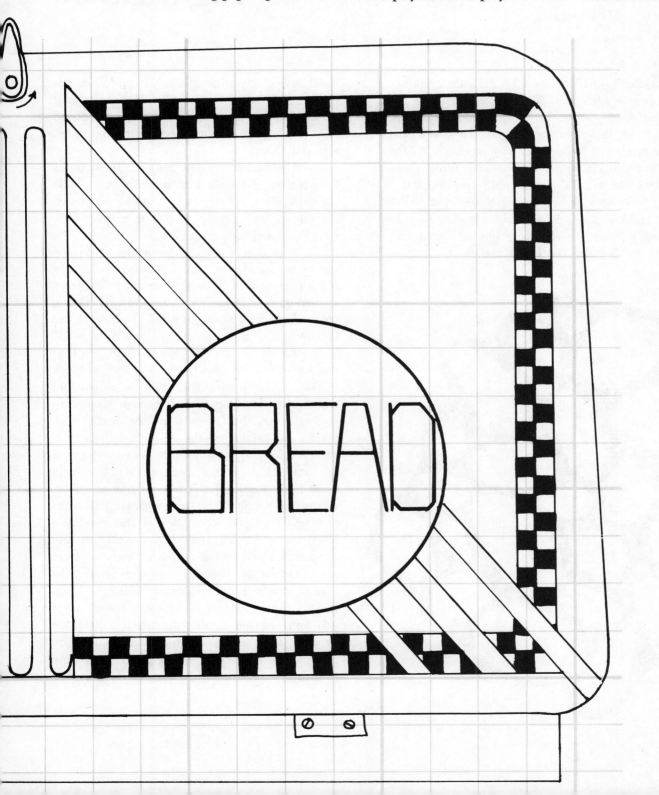

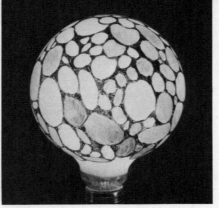

Shown in color on page 10

Light Bulbs

Globe light bulbs are a bit difficult to marker because—round and slippery as they are—it's a bit hard to control the drawing. Designs, therefore, have to be simple. However, the results always look pretty spectacular with the light shining through the colored glass. These light bulbs are 5½″ (13.75 cm.) in diameter.

Designs are given for these light bulbs, but frankly, there is no truly accurate way to transfer them. I strongly recommend that you take the bull by the horns and do them free-

hand, using the illustrations as guidelines for placing the basic shapes. The designs consist of little more than straight lines, circles and ellipses; they are meant to look somewhat rough and unfinished.

The easiest way to work on these bulbs is to screw the bulb into a lamp base while you're working. Then too, a template or stencil for the various sizes of circles is a great help (see Tools and Tips, page 23).

This design should be centered on the top or crown of the bulb. Draw the outlines in black marker and fill in with bright colors for a stained-glass effect. Remember to use strong colors that won't wash out when the light shines through.

To do the design shown here, start at the top center of the bulb and, with a black marker, draw circles and ellipses of random sizes quite close together as though they were paving stones. Fill in between the circles with black, and color in the circles with bright, strong colors. If you want to leave a part of the bulb clear at the bottom to get a little more light, finish off the bottom row of circles somewhat evenly. The accompanying illustration will give you some idea of the technique used, though you'll see as you work on this slippery subject, you're somewhat on your own.

On some brands of globe lamps the marker tends to intermittently stick or clog, due to the protective coating on the glass. If you find yourself in this predicament, it helps to work fast and to clean off the marker by coloring on a piece of scrap paper from time to time.

Shown in color on page 9

Frosted Globe Bulb

Frosted glass is a delight to work on. Not only does the marker color go on beautifully, but the frosting gives the color a lovely iridescence. This type of globe is a bit hard to locate, but the results are worth the search. In color and motif, the design imitates the art glass style of the Twenties. This globe is 8″ (20 cm.) in diameter.

For an authentic Art-Glass effect, marker the entire bulb first in one color—this globe is a very classic art-glass ochre color. To get the best results, start at the neck of the bulb and work upward in long, vertical overlapping strokes, carefully covering the whole surface.

Now enlarge the pattern, trace and transfer it. Determine the top center of the bulb and start the pattern at this point, going right over the color already applied. We used rather dark shades of blue, green and brown to complete the color scheme.

[73]

Mirror

Markered mirrors look wonderful. Here is a "boudoir table" design with a mirror in the center—good for last-minute makeup touchups if you hang it in your hall. Markers are also good for camouflaging old mirrors which have become spotted or frosted with age.

A couple of pointers. The slick mirror surface makes it very difficult to transfer designs; dressmaker's carbon seems to work best. As with any glass surface, only strong colors will show up well. Also, color will not adhere permanently to the surface until it is sprayed with a finish coat, so color carefully, being careful not to smear what you've already done. If you do make a mistake, you can in this instance "erase" the marker with a little water or nail polish remover on a tissue.

Start by drawing the small round "mirror" in the center. To do this, improvise a compass (as described on page 23). Place a couple of small pieces of masking tape in the center of the intended circle for the point of the compass to grip. Now, draw two concentric circles—the ones shown here are 7¾″ (19.5 cm.) and 8½″ (21.25 cm.) in diameter. Mirror dimensions (excluding frame) are 11½″ x 24″ (28.75 x 60 cm.). You can also make the circles (as I did) by using two bowls or flowerpots (or whatever) of the diameters you need. Or cut cardboard circles to size.

Next, draw in the paraphernalia on the "dressing table." Start from the foreground and work back toward the mirror, building up behind the objects in front. Color in the black outlines carefully with very strong colors. The frame of the "mirror" should be colored.

To do the vertical stripes in the background, start at a random point along the top edge of the mirror and, using a ruler to guide you, marker a vertical stripe of one color, running from the top of the mirror down to the dressing table. Run a line of a second color alongside this stripe, and a third line of yet another color alongside the second stripe. Now leave a little space and repeat.

You might try white marker for one of the colors, as shown here; it is actually opaque and masks out whatever it covers. The white marker needs a little time to dry, so take care not to smear. Red and blue were the other colors used for the background stripes, and red for the mirror frame. Consult your cosmetics for suggestions on coloring all the stuff on the "dressing table."

If your mirror has a square or rectangular frame, like the one shown, repeat the stripe pattern, or a variation of it, on the frame. To make sure the lines connect properly at the corners, make a pencil mark as shown from the inside to the outside of each corner.

Now the markered area must be sprayed with a couple of thin coats of plastic spray. The spray will leave a light film, so you must mask the viewing area of the "mirror." The simplest way to do this is to cut a circle out of cardboard the same diameter as the inner circle of the "mirror." Now, fasten this circle lightly in place over the "mirror" with a couple of masking-tape loops on the back of the cardboard. After you have sprayed the markered part, remove the cardboard.

Shown in color on page 11

Picture Frames

Templates like those mentioned on page 23 were used to do this very geometric Art Deco style frame. Lacking a template, it would be very simple to cut stencils for the main shapes. Start the frame by drawing the two black lines which run around the entire frame. All other motifs are placed along this line for easy layout.

Black and emerald green were the only colors used; you might prefer a more ambitious color scheme.

Floral frame (opposite): Here is a very inexpensive plastic picture frame, which after

Shown in color on page 13

Draw these lines first

ten minutes' effort looks pretty fancy. The secret of any simple project like this is that even the smallest amount of effort enhances it. Sometimes the more dull or pedestrian the object, the more spectacular the markered results.

The inside and outside rims of this frame are colored dark green. The rest is basically a series of dots and dashes. A running section of the pattern is given here. You can trace and transfer it, or you can do it freehand, which might be quicker and easier.

The important things to remember: Do the long dashes and big dots in a pale color and do them first, so the darker colors can be

used over them. For each side of the frame, start from the sides and work toward the middle. Keep the pattern symmetrical as you work toward the middle, and as you close in, work the pattern out so that you come out even. (If you look closely at the photo of this frame, you will see that the top and bottom patterns are actually different, but both are symmetrical.)

Triangles and dots (page 78): The trick to making something like this nondescript picture frame look like something special is to use very fanciful colors, very simple design ele-

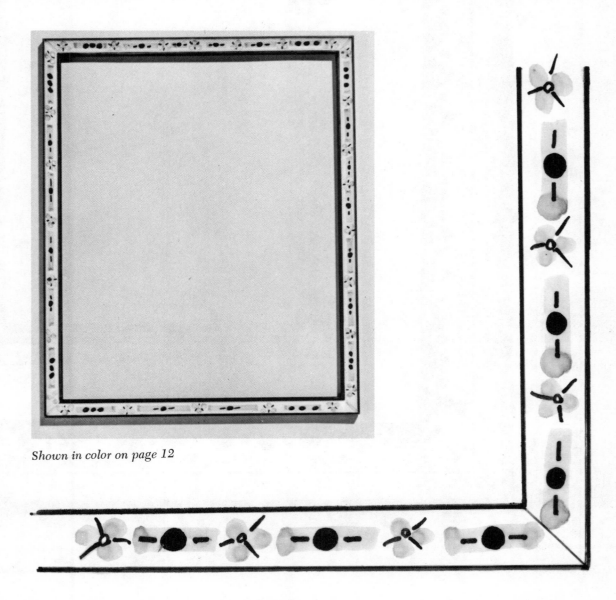

Shown in color on page 12

ments, and, most important, to delineate any crevasses or detail in the frame molding with dark fine-line markers.

Work with the fine-line marker first, filling in any grooves or detail. Skim the surfaces of other areas with bright, clear colors—use a different color for each area for the best definition. If there are any flat areas large enough, add detail with other colors as we did here with the stripes on the outside edge of the frame and the triangles and dots on the inside edge. Draw these freehand as they should in any case fit your frame. We used a bright blue fine-line marker to fill in the narrow grooves and did the rest in shocking pink, yellow, bright blue and orange.

Shown in color on page 10

Plaques

Shown in color on page 10

Hobby and craft stores sell these plain wooden plaques in many shapes and sizes, prefinished. They can be turned into any number of decorative household items. The ones shown here are going on my vegetable bin, but you might make a plaque with the family name on it for the front door of your house, for a child's room, as decorative labels for cabinets or drawers, etcetera. These plaques are 5½" (13.75 cm.) high.

Make a tracing-paper pattern of the basic motif to the size you need and transfer it to your plaque, placing it where it looks best. Then marker the background color around the main shape. The plaques we used have a nice, wide, beveled edge, which we markered in a darker color. We also patterned the edges a bit with short stripes in a still darker shade. Do the vegetable motifs next, using a black fine-line marker and other colors. Use nature as your guide.

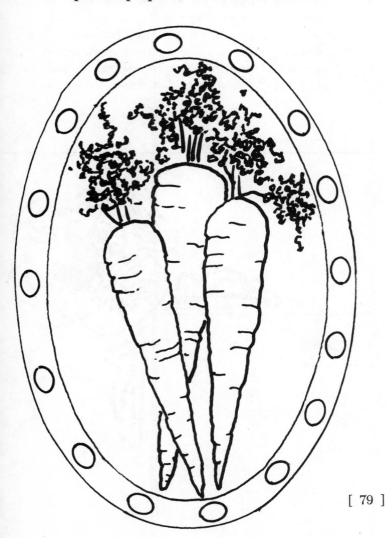

[79]

Shown in color on page 10

Picture Mats

Store-bought picture frames usually come with rather flimsy pre-cut mats, which can be markered, adding immeasurably to almost any framed picture. Great gifts can be made by markering mats on framed photos or mementos of special occasions. The frames shown here came with colored mats, but you can also cut

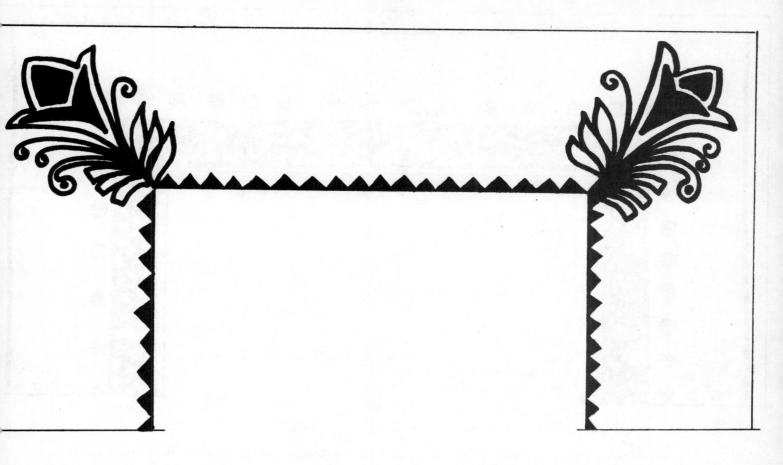

Shown in color on page 11

your own mat from colored paper, or buy pre-cut colored mats which you can get at most art and photography supply stores.

If you cut your own mat, the outside dimensions should be just a sliver smaller than the given dimensions of the frame; allow approximately ¼″ (6 mm.) all around the actual picture being framed.

The motifs on the mats shown here could be used on almost any picture; yet they were copied directly from elements in the subjects being framed—lovely labels from French products sent to me by a friend in Paris. Taking inspiration from the color or subject matter of the picture you're framing is a good idea; it lends coherence and unity, and makes good design sense.

The patterns given here are for half of each of the mats. If you're tracing the design, do the top half, then turn the mat around to do the bottom. If you're working on mats of a different size from those shown here, the easiest

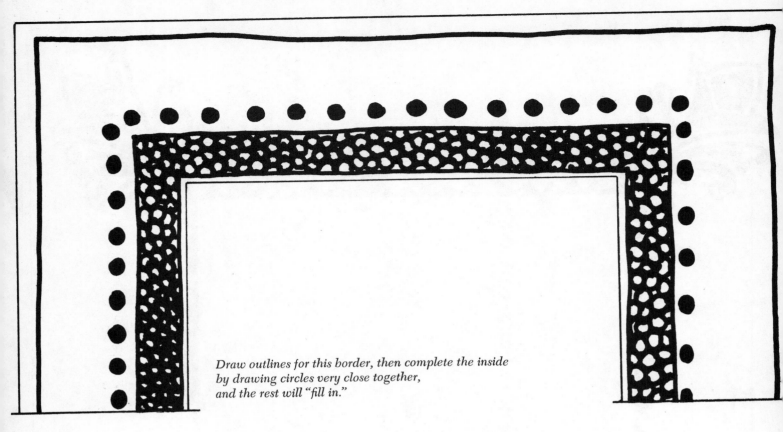

*Draw outlines for this border, then complete the inside
by drawing circles very close together,
and the rest will "fill in."*

way of adapting your design is to first do the parts of the design which go all around the mat (no pattern is needed) and then make

tracing-paper patterns of the corner motifs to the size you need and transfer them to your mat.

Shown in color on page 12

Wood Molding Strips

Shown in color on page 11

Pressed wood molding strips in various patterns and widths are sold in many hardware stores and lumber yards. They're very decorative, and easy to marker. Markered molding strips can be added to the edges of a plain table, along the edges of drawers or cabinet doors, bookshelves, etcetera. They look great.

Although the patterns on these strips are usually quite detailed, they can be quickly colored by running the marker across the top of the raised areas, and then filling in the small grooves and crevasses with fine-line markers for definition.

On this project, I recommend that you seal the wood first to guard against bleed in the small, detailed areas you'll be working on. A light coat of a plastic spray such as Varathane should be sufficient.

As a rule, it is best to use dark colors to fill in the deep grooves and crevasses: they give more definition to the pattern of the molding. As for coloring the molding, your choice should be based on the decor of the room or the mood you want to create. Two different color schemes can entirely change the feeling of the same molding pattern.

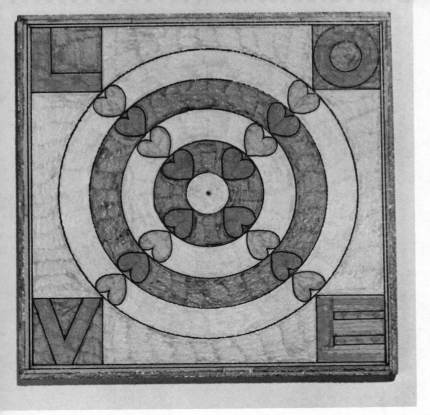

Shown in color on page 10

Dart Boards

Beaverboard—a ½″ (1.25 cm.) thick composition board—comes with one surface already primed with flat white paint, ready for markering and ideal for making bulletin boards or game boards for playing darts. It's available at lumber yards and some hardware stores; if you're lucky and if you don't need a specific size, you can buy a couple of scrap pieces rather than have it cut to order. Boards are 18″ (45 cm.) square.

The only pointer in working on this flat, primed surface is that the colors will tend to look chalky and dull, so choose bright, intense colors unless you like the soft look. Or spray with a coat of Varathane or other finish before you start.

Two suggestions are given here for dartboard games. You could, of course, just copy a regulation dart board, but these boards are a little different and more decorative, and might be more fun to play. You can improvise your own rules, but here's one suggestion for each game:

Love board: Make an X as shown in the illustration to connect the four corners to determine the center of the board. Using a regular dime-store compass with a black fine-line marker wedged and taped into it (see Tools and Tips, page 23), rule a circle with a 1″ (2.5 cm.) radius. Extend the compass 1½″ (3.75 cm.) more and rule the next circle. Each of the next three circles is again 1½″ larger. Draw a double border ⅜″ (9 mm.) and ½″ (1.25 cm.) from the edge all around. Next, do the letters in the four corners, using the point where the dotted line touches the perimeter of the circle as the corner of the square. Draw in the hearts, using the dotted line as your center line for each heart. You may want to make a stencil for doing the hearts.

The love board is done almost entirely in shades of pink and blue, but you might prefer bright red Valentine hearts.

Set a number of points to win the game (200 or 300). The outer circle counts 5 points, the next 10, then 15, 25, and 50 points for the

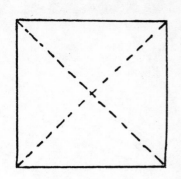

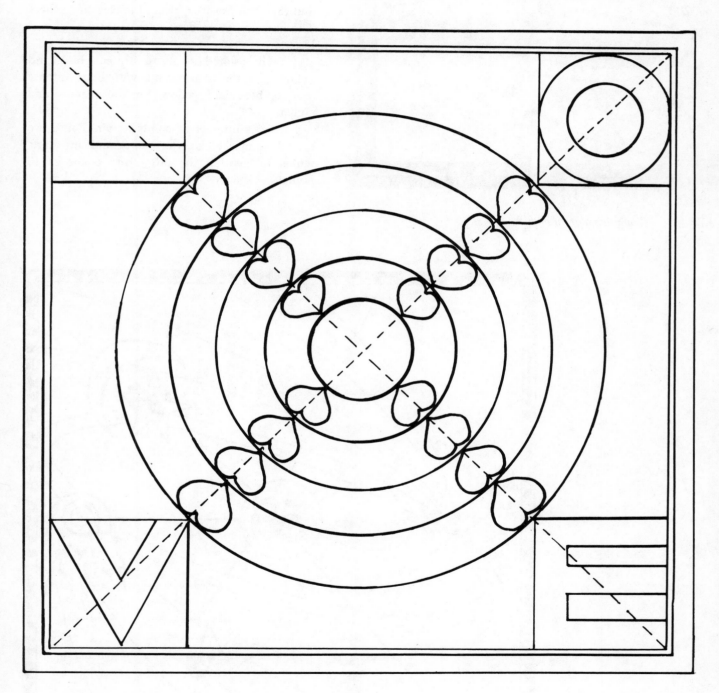

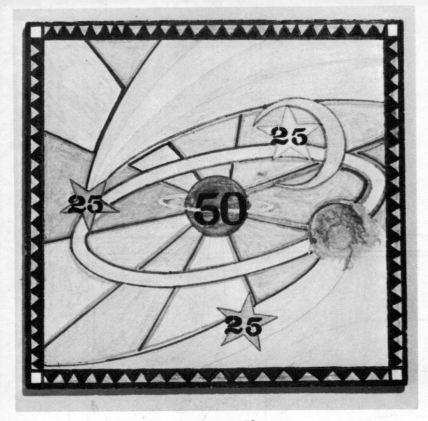

Shown in color on page 12

bull's-eye. If you land on a heart, it counts double the number of points for that circle. Landing on L-O-V-E might be a bonus two points.

Solar system board: Draw the border design. Enlarge the pattern to the size you need and then transfer it by using the carbon method. The numbers were done with the aid of stencil letters.

The colors here are mostly pale blues and yellows for the background, with more intense orange, blue and yellow for the planets and comet.

Set a number of points to win. Points are scored as marked on the board, and any darts which fall within the large ring count as 10 points.

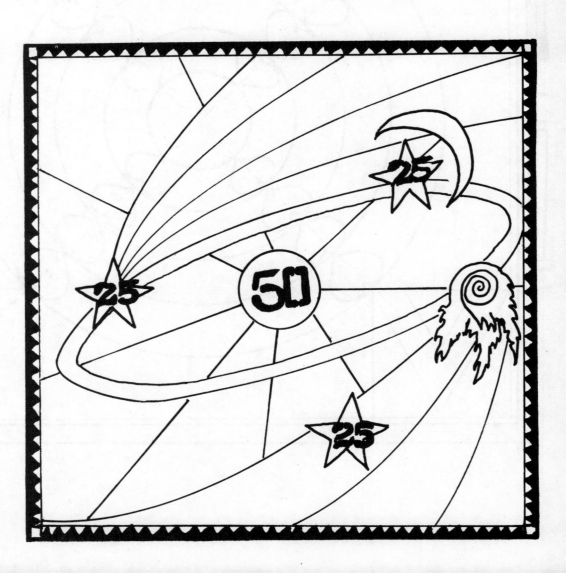

Knobs

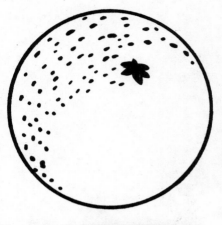

Small, decorative unfinished wood hardware that usually doesn't get much attention can be turned into something unique with your markers. Cabinet knobs, drawer knobs and handles, door knobs, etcetera, are especially good targets.

Take for your subject matter something related to what's in the drawer or cabinet or something which goes with the shape of the fixture. The tomato and the orange shown here would look well in a kitchen; the profiles would go in a study or a bedroom. You might number, or letter, knobs with dime-store stencils, or key them to what's inside the drawer or cabinet (glasses, cups, plates, etcetera).

Use the carbon method to transfer the designs, making your pattern the size that you need. Make sure you color all around the edges—neatness counts—and spray with a couple of coats of plastic spray, since they'll be getting quite a bit of wear.

Fairly strong colors were used on the knobs shown here, but you should take inspiration from the colors used in your room. You could do the same designs using pastel colors and get a very different effect.

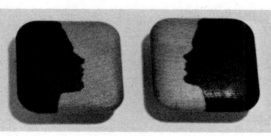

Shown in color on page 10

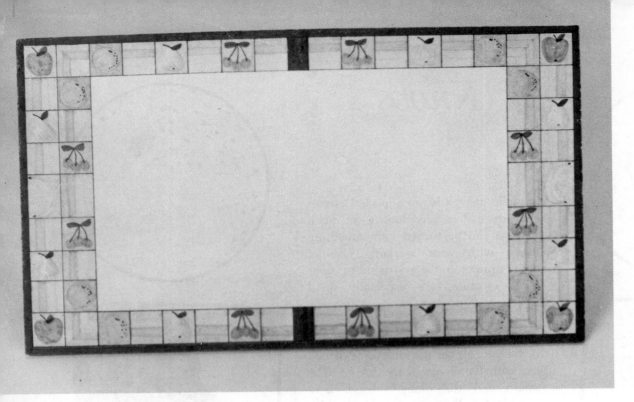

Shown in color on page 9

A		O		P		C			C		P		O		A
	O													O	
P															P
	C													C	
B															B
	C													C	
P															P
	O													O	
A		O		P		C			C		P		O		A

Bulletin Board

Bulletin boards markered to go with your own room—or your own interests—are easy to make with beaverboard. The one here is based on a border of 2″ (5 cm.) squares inside a ½″ (1.25 cm.) border; full size of the bulletin board is 19″ x 33″ (47.5 x 82.5 cm.). Every other square has a small fruit design (for which you might want to make stencils). The squares between the fruit motifs are bands of freehand stripes repeating four of the colors used for the backgrounds of the fruit motifs—aqua, pink, blue and beige.

The illustration shows the layout of the squares and the placement of the fruit (A=apple, O=orange, P=pear, C=cherries, B=banana). Every other square has stripes. Draw the stripes by hand, using a generous quarter of the width of each square for each color, so that the colors overlap and blend. Color the other squares and then color the fruit. Use a spray plastic finish.

If you need to adjust the pattern to fit the size of your board, you can do so by adding or subtracting squares. Just be sure that you keep the pattern symmetrical—that is, you add or subtract the squares at the middle of each side, and work the layout of fruit in toward the center.

Bulletin boards are good decorative items for children's and teenagers' rooms, and a good incentive to a sense of organization. Try a motif of special interest to them.

Do these stripes freehand

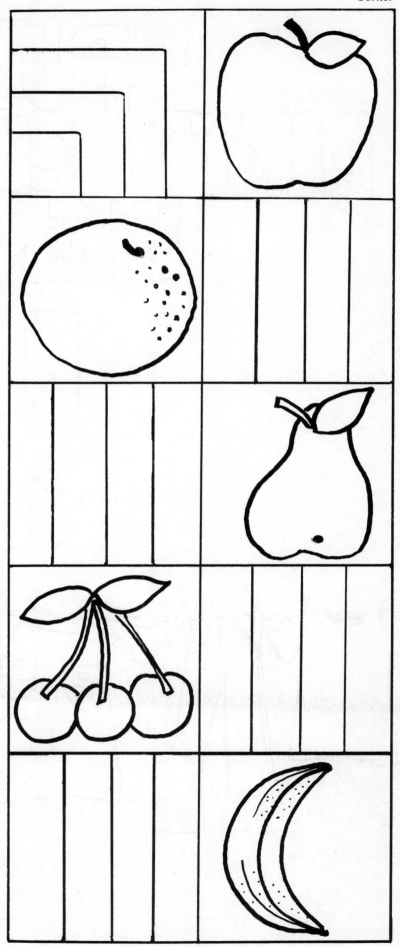

Laundry Bag

Marker a plain laundry bag and it's a portable hamper nice enough to hang in the bathroom—also decorative and presentable enough to take to the apartment-house laundry room, or to the laundromat. These long, narrow bags, 17″ x 33″ (42.5 x 82.5 cm.) seem to be a staple item in many hardware and dime stores; any drawstring bag will serve the purpose.

Use the carbon method to transfer the pattern, enlarging it first to the correct size. The fabric is thin, so use paper or cardboard between the layers to arrest bleed.

To color, do the clothes the same colors as your own clothes, and be sure to marker the detergent box in bright primary colors. The tiles behind the washing machine could match the colors of your own bathroom or laundry room.

If you carry your laundry bag around to public places—laundry room or laundromat—marker your name or a monogram on it for identification.

Shown in color on page 9

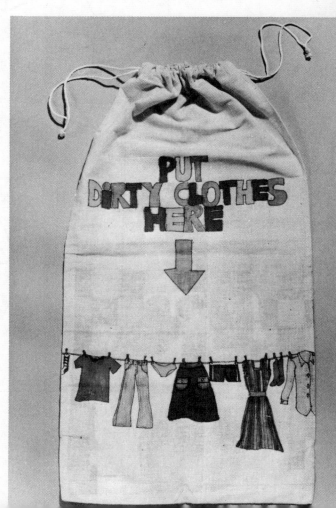

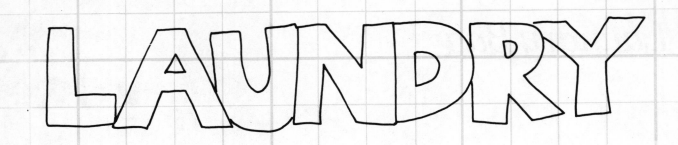

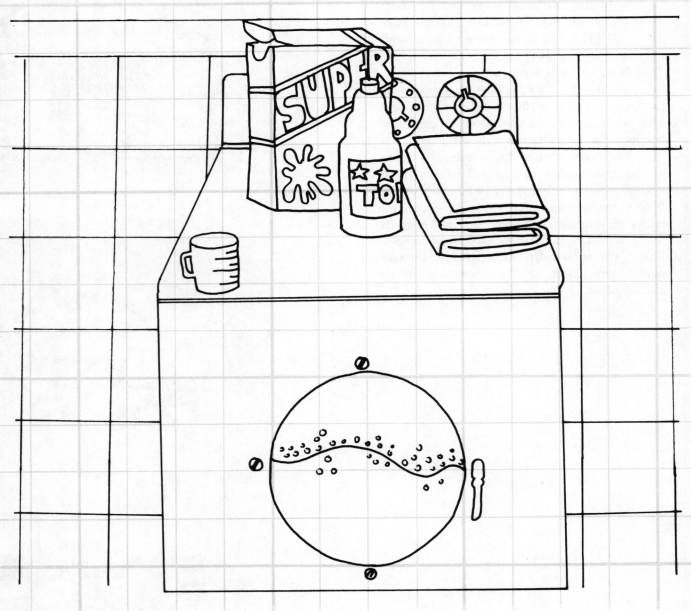

Continue tiles pattern out to sides of bag

Placemats

Plastic placemats like these sell in many dime and variety stores for about a quarter apiece. There's no limit to the design possibilities—you can copy the design of your tablecloth or your kitchen wallpaper. They can be personalized and you can even change the design from time to time for variety, or for a special occasion or a party. When you buy them, they come with rather prosaic designs on them, but the backs are blank, so your paper is already cut to size. These placemats are 11″ x 14″ (27.5 x 35 cm.).

The first step is to remove the sealed-in design. Turn the placemat over so the reverse side is facing you and, using an X-acto knife, a mat knife or a single-edge razor blade, slit carefully through only the back thickness of the plastic along one of the short sides just inside the border. Remove the inside sheet. Then slip the new design inside the plastic frame, so that it will be facing up; be sure no dust gets inside. Seal the slit with a strip of invisible mending tape.

Enlarge the pattern to the size you need and transfer the design to the placemat. A note on transferring the designs: Since there are few black outlines on these motifs, transfer the designs *lightly*, using the carbon method, because the pencil lines will not disappear entirely under the light-colored markers.

On these "breakfast" placemats, we have a placemat within a placemat, with complete table settings. Colors are pretty much true to life—a red apple, an orange, orange juice, etcetera—and the "placemats" were left white. The area outside the placemats is markered in freehand stripes to look like a tablecloth— one in blue, the other in yellow.

Here we have a hamburger on a blue checked tablecloth and a hot dog on a red checked tablecloth with very little color used elsewhere.

[93]

Shown in color on pages 9 and 12

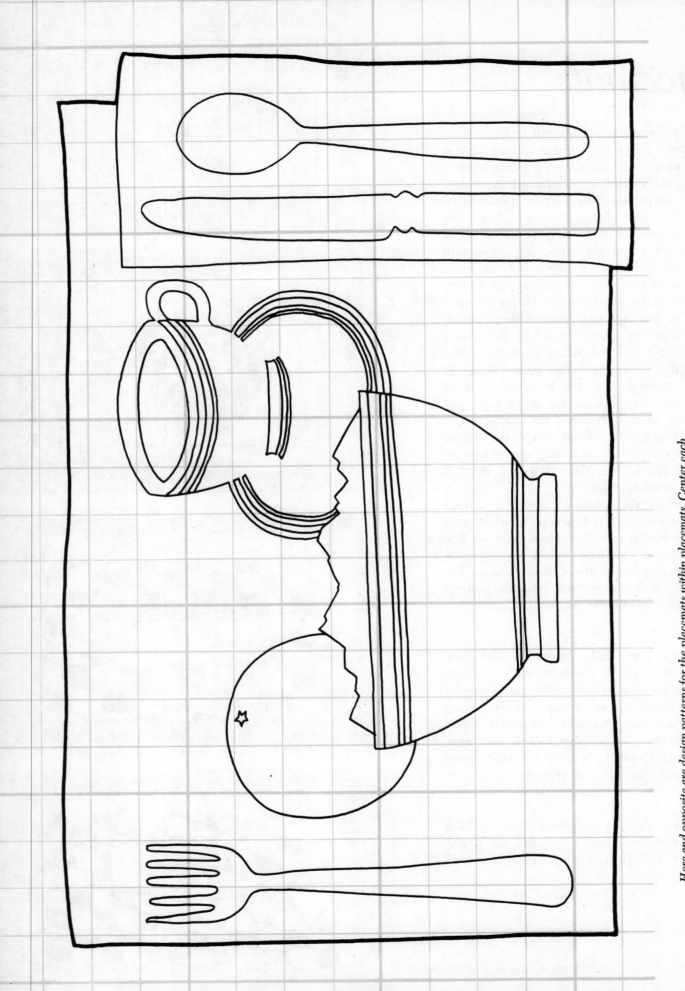

Here and opposite are design patterns for the placemats within placemats. Center each design on your placemat. The only black outline is around the mat and napkin; the other lines just indicate shapes to be filled in with color. The background—i.e., the "tablecloth" shown in the photos on page 93—is just freehand vertical stripes going out to the edges of your design.

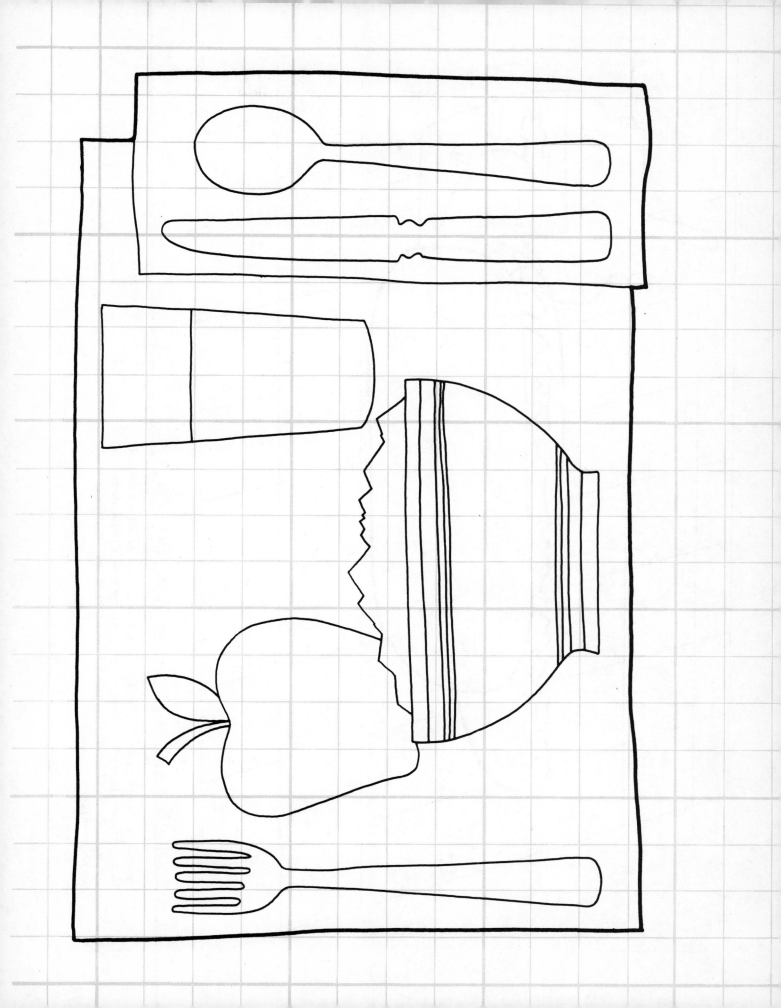

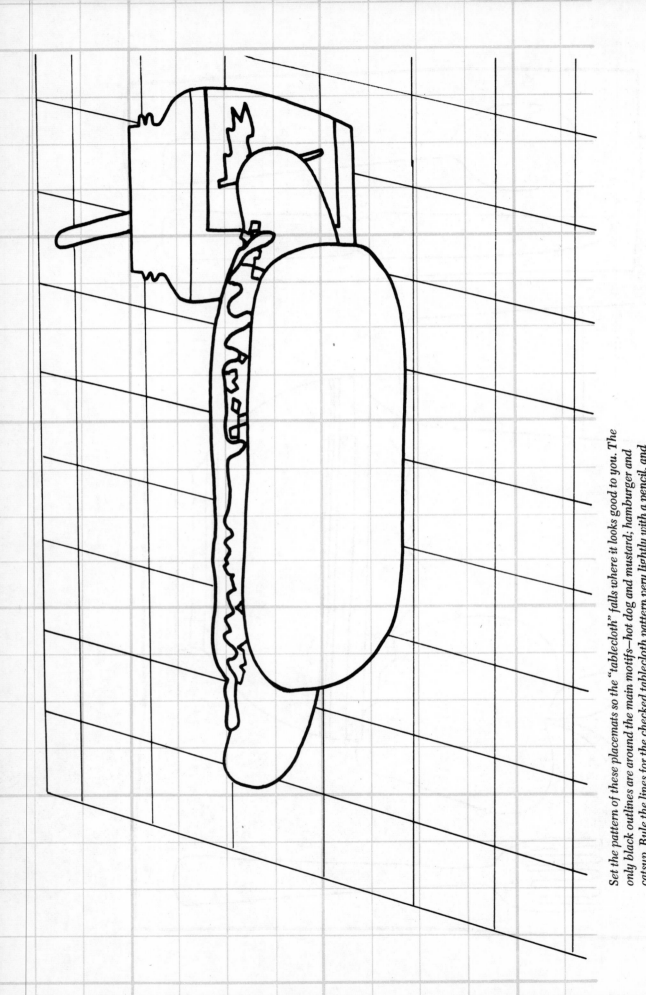

Set the pattern of these placemats so the "tablecloth" falls where it looks good to you. The only black outlines are around the main motifs—hot dog and mustard; hamburger and catsup. Rule the lines for the checked tablecloth pattern very lightly with a pencil, and fill in every other square with your chosen color. Don't worry about perfect outlines— working freehand with a wide-tip marker will give a more rumpled, clothlike effect (see photos on page 93).

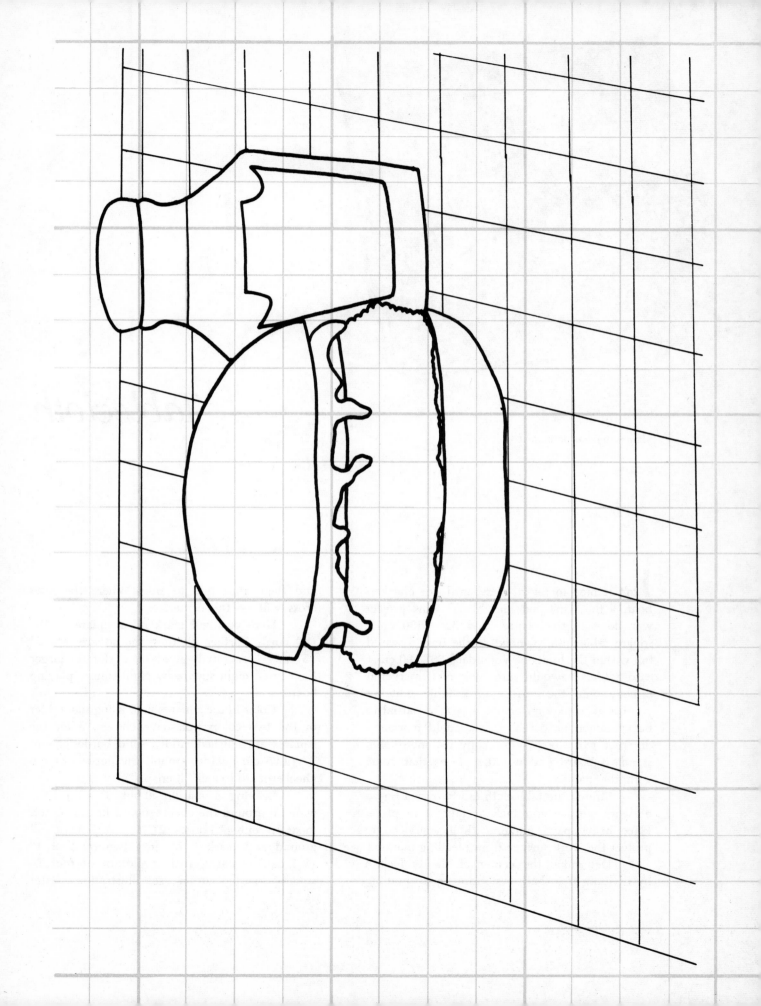

Shown in color on page 13

Tablecloth

Isn't it nice to see a chessboard (or checkerboard) that isn't red and black? This project was done in the center of a 52″ (130 cm.) square tablecloth, planned so the design would fall within the limits of a standard 36″ (90 cm.) card table. It would also look nice markered directly onto the surface of a table—whether you use it to play on or not. If you're partial to backgammon or parchesi, you could marker a different game board—just copy the motif of a standard board and use the pieces that come with the game.

Stretch the tablecloth tautly over a board or work surface and tack or tape it in place. Place heavy paper underneath if you need to protect the work surface from bleeding markers.

Determine the center of the tablecloth by dividing it in half, first from top to bottom, and then from side to side. Where the lines cross will be the center.

Here you will mark off a square of 16″ (40 cm.). Further dividing the square into 2″ (5 cm.) blocks will give you a slightly larger than usual eight-square by eight-square playing board.

Color in the squares first, using the lighter of the two colors you have chosen. After the squares are finished, add a solid border, about ½″ (1.25 cm.) wide, around the outside of the checkerboard to make it crisp.

Leaving a margin about 3″ (7.5 cm.) wide all around the checkerboard in the center, measure out a border 2″ (5 cm.) wide all around and mark it off into two rows of 1″ (2.5 cm.) squares, with a pattern of four 2″ squares in each corner (see illustration). After

[98]

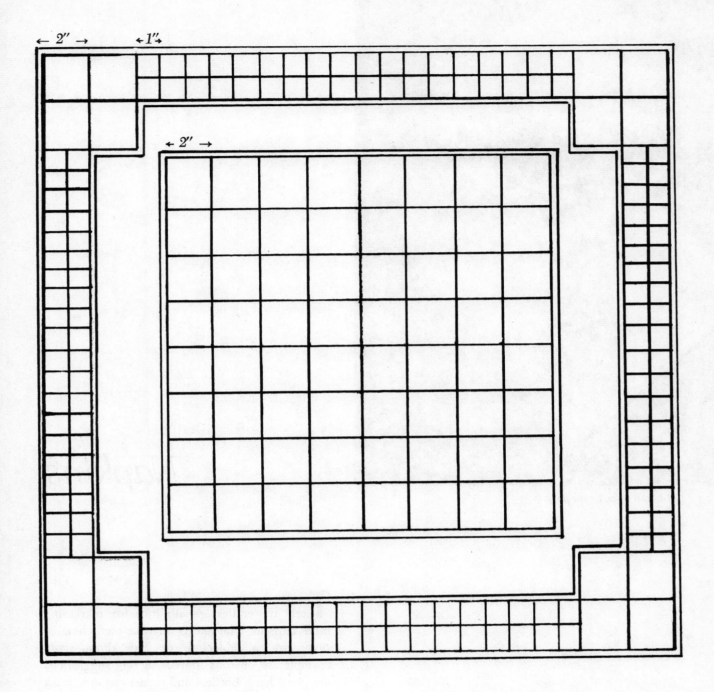

you rule and color them with your markers, again add a border all around the edges of this motif to tighten up the edges and unify it with the center motif.

The color scheme here is very simple—just dark green and lavender on the blue cloth.

Your choice will depend on your own background color and the color scheme of the room you will use it in.

Note: If you prefer, you can draw the whole design first, before you begin coloring in with the markers.

Shown in color on page 9

Napkins

There are endless possibilities for markering table napkins. The motifs on your own china or silverware, a tablecloth or your dining-room curtains are obvious sources. A few suggestions are given here. Borders and corner patterns work best, and take very little time.

Trace and transfer the patterns using the carbon method. As napkins will get considerable washing, be sure to test your colors first for fastness (see Markering on Fabric, page 25).

The bunch of purple grapes looks lovely on the blue napkin, and the red strawberry is perfect for the pink one. Take care that your color choice goes with your background color.

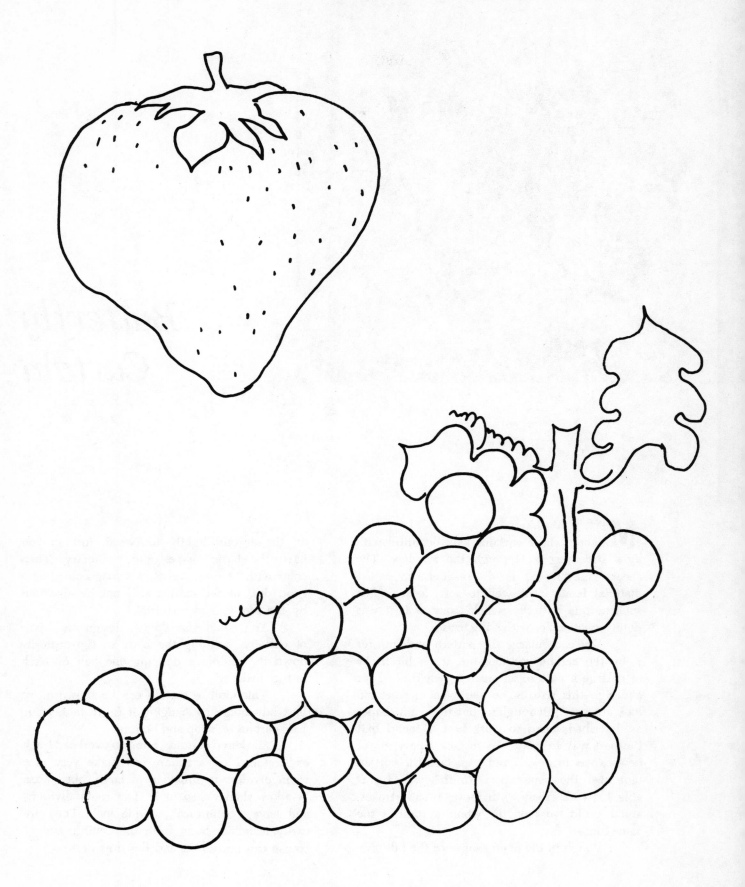

Butterfly Curtain

Markered sheer curtains look beautiful with light streaming in through the window. The sheer, gauzy fabric bleeds considerably, so the material lends itself well to soft, loose motifs such as this butterfly which looks as if it was done in watercolor with a big brush.

You can enlarge the pattern and transfer it by the carbon method, but it's a bit tricky to enlarge a pattern as much as you'd need for a design this size. Since you want a freehand look anyway, just roughing out the main shapes as described seems to work best. I found that the best way to work was to tack a covering of newspapers to a wall and then tack the curtain taut over the newspapers. In this way I was able to work freely with loose, broad strokes, and I could work on the whole curtain at the same time.

Rough in the main shapes of the butterfly on the curtain lightly in pencil, just so you have the basic shapes and symmetry. Then color with bold strokes. Use strong colors, as a good deal of the marker will not be absorbed by the flimsy, slick material.

You could also do the design on a pair of curtains, splitting the body of the butterfly down the middle and doing one half on each of the curtains.

This kind of curtain can be shown off to best advantage by hanging it fairly taut, using cafe curtain rods top and bottom.

Markered curtains, hung on overhead track or stretched on a frame, can make very nice room dividers to break up a large, open area. Window shades also make fine room dividers, and have a whimsical, unique look. They are easily installed, hung from the ceiling, and of course can be run up and down as desired.

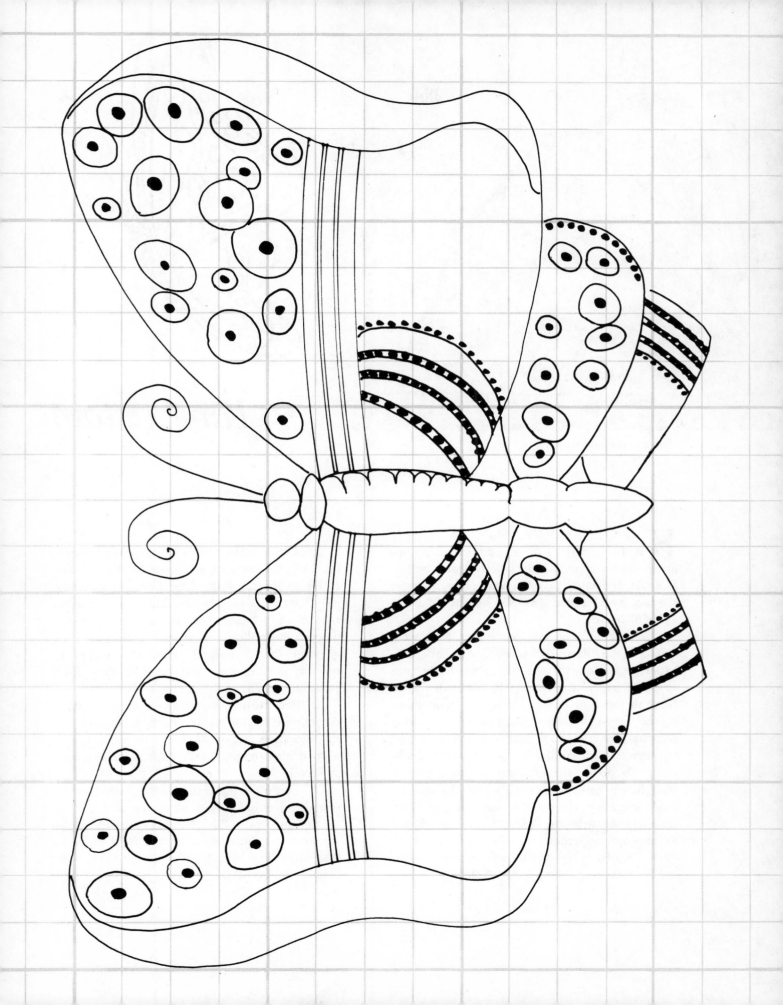

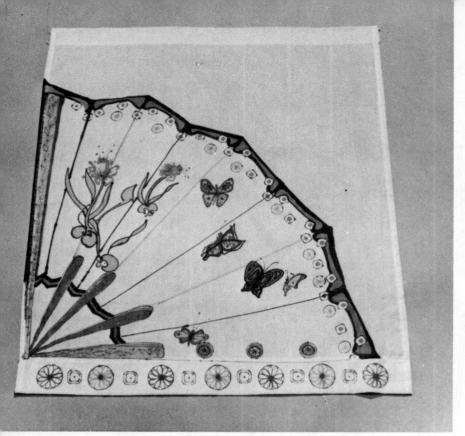

Shown in color on page 12

Fan Curtain

ere is a pretty pair of curtains in a Japanese fan motif with lots of flowers and butterflies. As the curtains open and close, so does the fan. Each curtain size used here is 30″ x 35″ (75 x 87.5 cm.).

Tack or tape one curtain to your work surface (the illustration shows both, but it is easier to work with one at a time). Be sure to place papers underneath to catch the bleed through the thin fabric. Draw the basic shape of the fan—you'll have to improvise a string compass (as described under Tools and Tips on page 23) to handle this large quarter-circle.

To divide the fan into sections, draw a straight line across the points where the quarter-circle intersects the sides of the fan (see illustration). Measure the line and mark it off into an appropriate number of equal sections. Then draw lines from the center point of the fan out to the perimeter of the quarter-circle.

Transfer the motifs by the carbon method. Full-size patterns are given for the flowers, and also for the butterflies; place them where they look most pleasing to you, using the illustration as a guide. When you have all the flowers, butterflies, border motifs, etcetera, then go over the "structural" lines of the fan in marker, making sure that none of these lines pass through any of the smaller motifs.

Red, turquoise and green were the main colors used on our yellow curtain. The lines of the fan itself are in brown. For curtains, it's a good idea to spray with a fabric sealant such as Scotchgard.

To do the matching curtain, turn the first completed curtain over, place the new curtain on top and trace this "flopped" pattern. Make sure you do the curtains in the right order so that when they hang together they form a half-circular fan as shown.

Full-size patterns for Fan Curtain, page 104

These are shown in color
on pages 9, 10, 11 and 13

Pillowcases

No need to hide these pillowcases under a bedspread—and no need to pay outrageous sums for printed pillowcases. Plain white pillowcases can be purchased in most dime stores, and they marker beautifully.

Pillowcases done in pairs are fun on a double bed. Or, instead of using expensive throw pillows, marker a bunch of pillows to throw on a day bed. A personalized pillowcase makes a good get-well gift for a sick friend. Or a good get-well craft project for an ailing child.

There are no special tricks to doing pillowcases. Remember to put something between the layers of fabric to keep the color from bleeding through to the back. Use the carbon method to transfer your designs, and tack or tape the pillowcase to your work surface. Be sure to center the design on the pillowcase, leaving an even border all around. When doing a pair of pillowcases, be sure you're markering them so that the flaps face in the right direction (see illustration, page 112).

When coloring pillowcases, treat them as a set if they are going to be on the same bed, and use the same color scheme so they look like they go together. The sun and moon pillowcases both have a dark blue sky, with the border and lettering done in blue, green and pink, and a lot of yellow in the central sun/moon motif.

The unifying element of the other set (shown at right) is the border of small squares all around both pillowcases. Even though they don't really match, using similar colors for both makes them look alike.

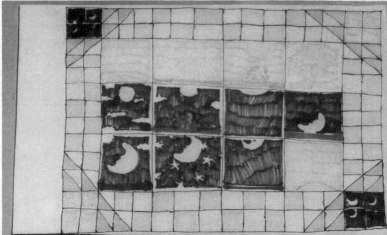

[107]

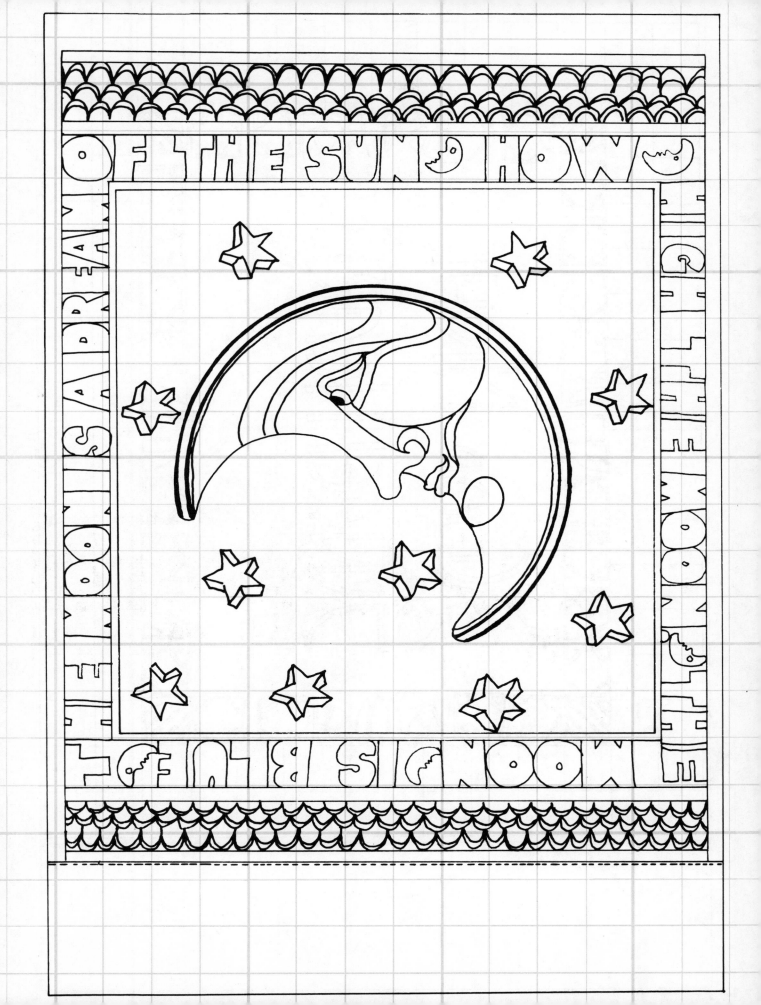

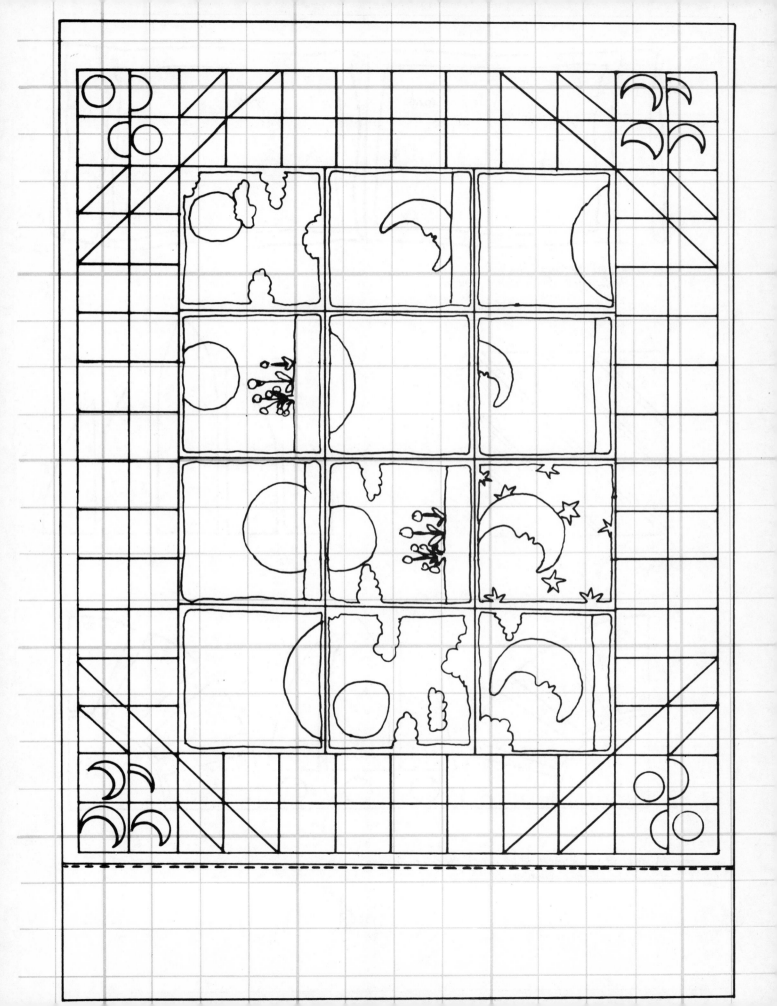

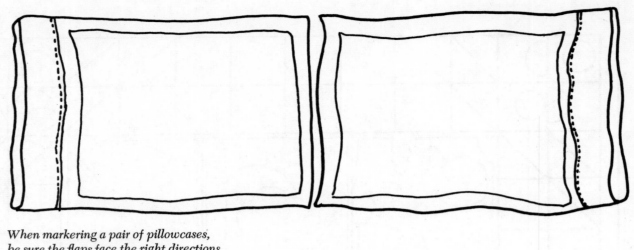

*When markering a pair of pillowcases,
be sure the flaps face the right directions*

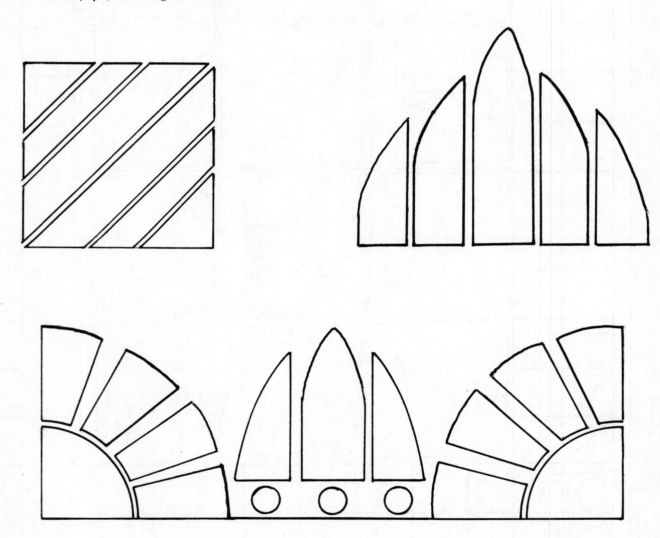

*(Above and opposite): Here are patterns for all the design elements
used in the pillowcase borders*

Shown in color on page 10

Invitations

Packets of sixteen envelopes and blank note forms sell in my neighborhood dime store for well under a dollar. It takes but a few minutes, using the simplest motifs, to turn them into unique party invitations or thank you notes.

To guard against bleed, work quickly and work with the note paper open and with something inside the envelope. The patterns given are full size, so you can use the carbon method to transfer them. These designs are meant to be quick and loose, so don't worry about duplicating the pattern exactly.

The color schemes were kept very simple and the motif on the invitation is repeated with some variation on the envelope: pink candles; green Christmas trees on a pale, snowy ground; a green olive with a red pimiento; and red, yellow and pink balloons.

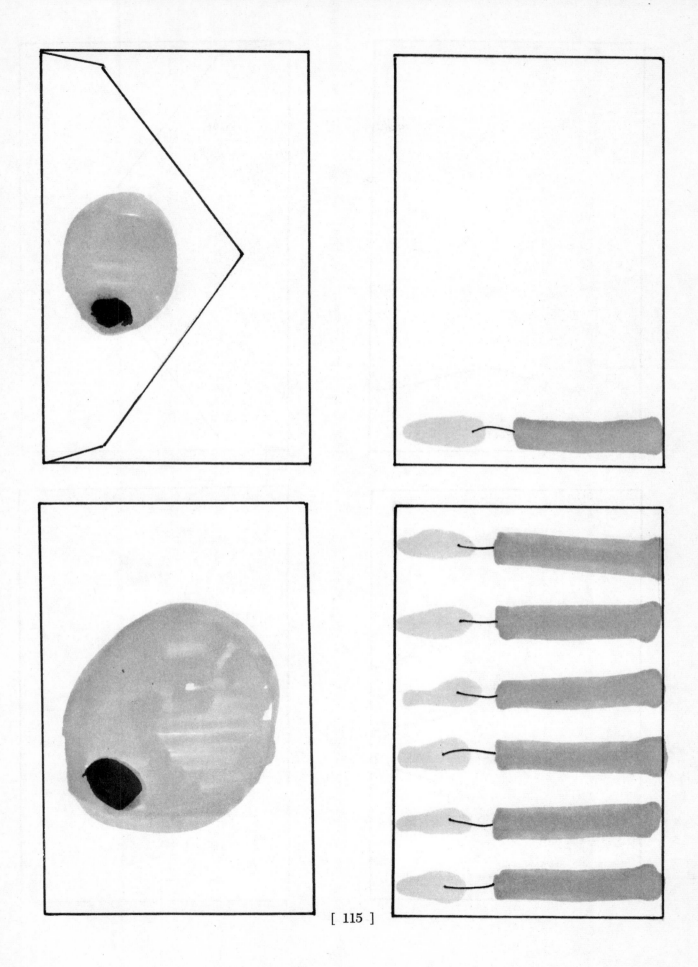

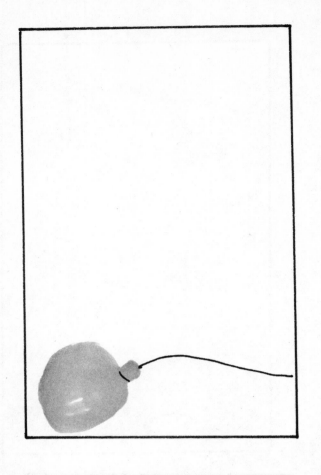

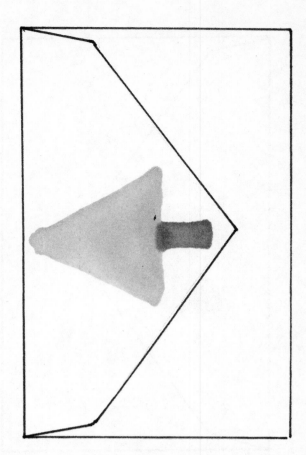

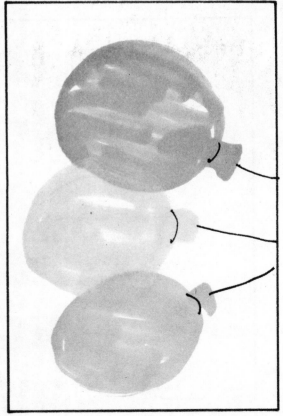

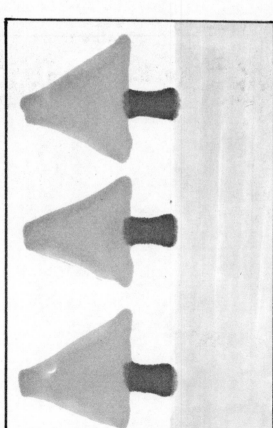

Stationery

Shown in color on pages 11 and 13

Using the simplest motifs, you can decorate and personalize plain stationery, making it uniquely your own. Simplicity of design is the key here, because you don't want to spend more than a few minutes on something which is so ephemeral. Should you settle on a motif you especially like, you can "mass produce" several sheets of stationery and envelopes in a matter of minutes.

The designs shown here are good examples of fast, decorative letterhead styles. You might also type your name or sign it with a flourish at the top of the page over the finished design. Another way is to monogram your initials using dime-store stencil letters.

Any variation of stripes, checks or dots goes very quickly (see illustration).

These patterns are meant to be allover motifs, so keep your colors light. When you do allover motifs, place a larger piece of scrap paper under the stationery so you can marker the entire width and length of the stationery without worrying about damaging what's underneath. Such motifs as the lips and the orange seem to look best centered at the top of the paper; on the envelope they can be placed on the front where the return address would go, or on the back flap. Again, pale colors look best: pink lips on pale pink stationery, the orange on orange stationery, a yellow lemon on yellow paper.

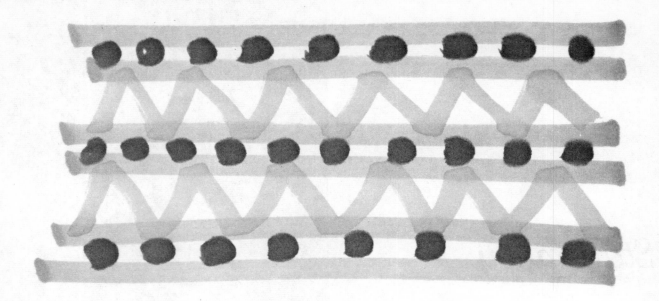

(Above and below):
Some simple line/dot patterns
suitable for note paper and stationery

For the lips, just pencil in the outline
very lightly, then color boldly with
marker in broad vertical stripes

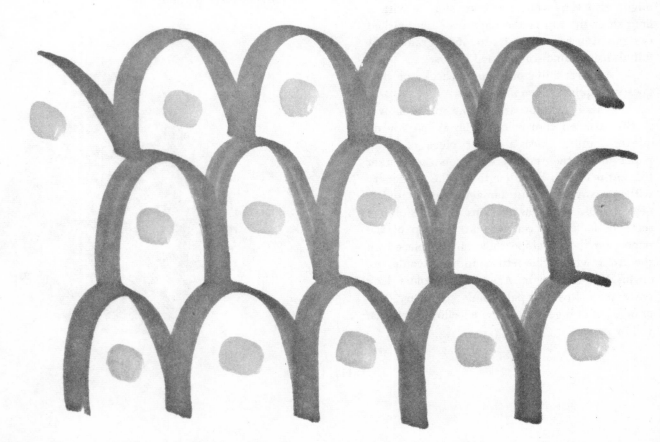

*See how you can vary criss-crossed lines
to give a checked or a plaid effect*

Shown in color on pages 10 and 12

Wrapping Paper

It takes longer to tie a fancy bow than it does to marker gift paper. Any kind of paper can be used—brown kraft paper, butcher paper, newspaper. No need to buy expensive gift wrap. I especially like the look of markered foil. The color goes on smooth and shiny, and the pressure of the marker actually "embosses" the foil as you work.

The easiest way to work is to wrap your gift first, holding the wrapping in place with tape. Then marker the already wrapped package. The designs given here are meant mostly for inspiration, but you can enlarge some of the main motifs using the carbon method and transfer them to your gift wrap.

No need to make an elaborate production of the coloring. Just a few colors will make any simple wrapping paper look very festive.

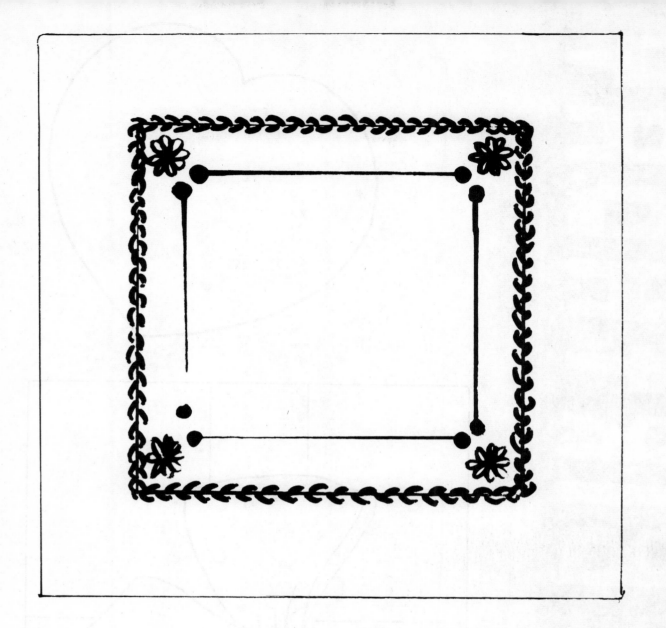

merry
X mas

Shown in color on pages 11, 12 and 13

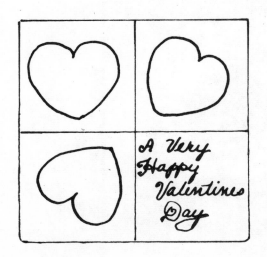

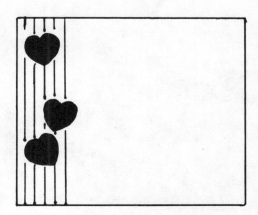

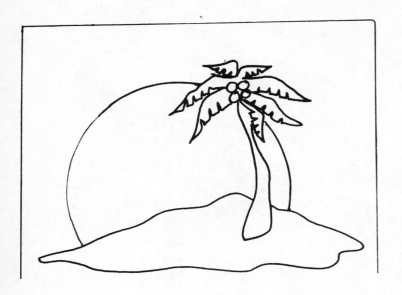

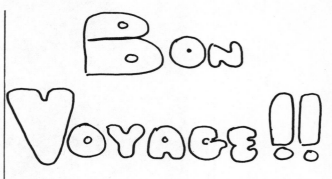

Shown in color on pages 10 and 11

CLOTHES AND ACCESSORIES

T-Shirts

T-shirts are my favorite marker project—fun to make, fun to give, fun to wear. Back in the days when I thought of markers as just an important business tool—for designing graphics work—I hit on the idea of making T-shirts as gifts for friends on special occasions. Now,

The shirts are shown in color on pages 14 and 15

there's hardly a thing I wouldn't marker, but T-shirts are still a sentimental favorite.

Nowadays, T-shirts are tremendously popular, and those you find in the store are either very expensive or everyone on the block has the same shirt. The T-shirts here are different and make wonderful gifts. I'm rather fond of fool-the-eye styles, as you can see here —T-shirts markered to look like sweaters, baseball shirts, etcetera. The possibilities are limitless—it's especially fun to marker a shirt that looks like the style of clothes worn by its owner.

I've found that the best way to work on T-shirts is to stretch them over a large piece of cardboard or masonite, or, better yet, a large pad of drawing paper. This holds the knit material taut as you work, and excess fabric at the sides and sleeves can be pulled around to the back of this work surface and held in place with masking tape. Another trick is to enlarge the T-shirt pattern to the correct size on a drawing pad. Now, stretch the T-shirt over the pad, and trace the pattern through the thin material with your markers. To do the back of the shirt, just untape the excess material from the back, pull it around to the front, and re-tape. Turn the shirt over and draw the back of the shirt.

Several T-shirt ideas are given here. Try making the same T-shirt for every member of your family. Dress *everyone* up in bikinis.

Note: Don't forget to test your colors (as described under Markering on Fabric on page 25).

When coloring T-shirts that are supposed to "fool the eye," I try to make the colors look as much like the real thing as possible. For example, the Mets T-shirt is done in the team colors. In doing shirts such as the cloud T-shirt or the torso T-shirt where there will be color on the sleeves, be sure to place the design so that no color goes under the armpits, where perspiration can cause the color to run.

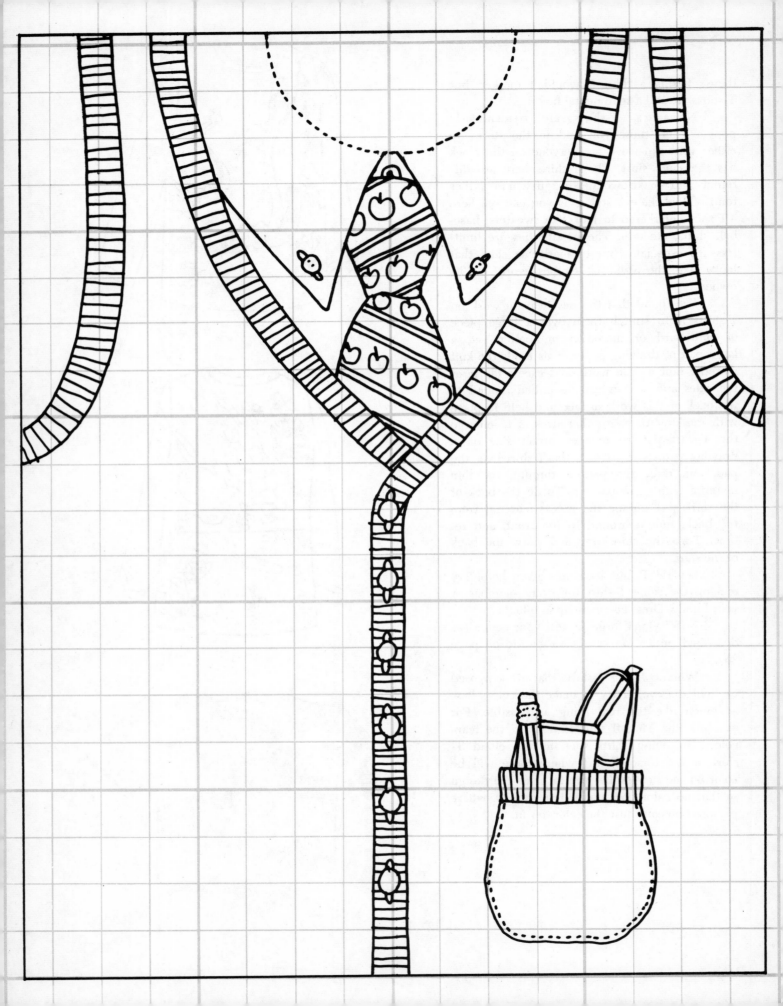

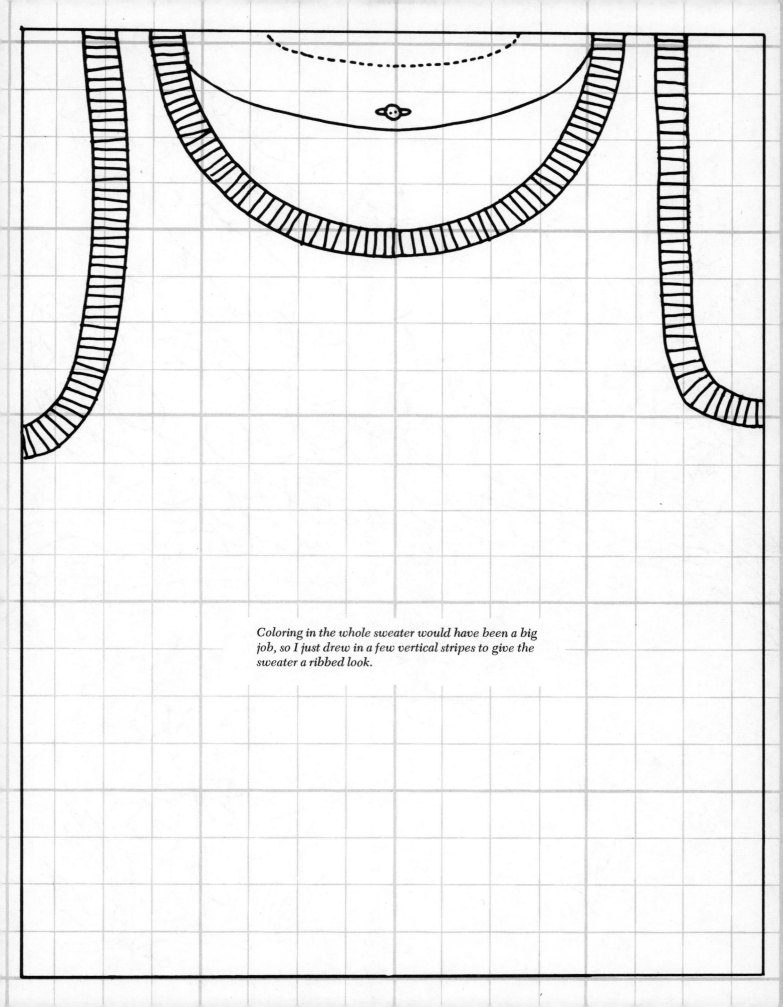

Coloring in the whole sweater would have been a big job, so I just drew in a few vertical stripes to give the sweater a ribbed look.

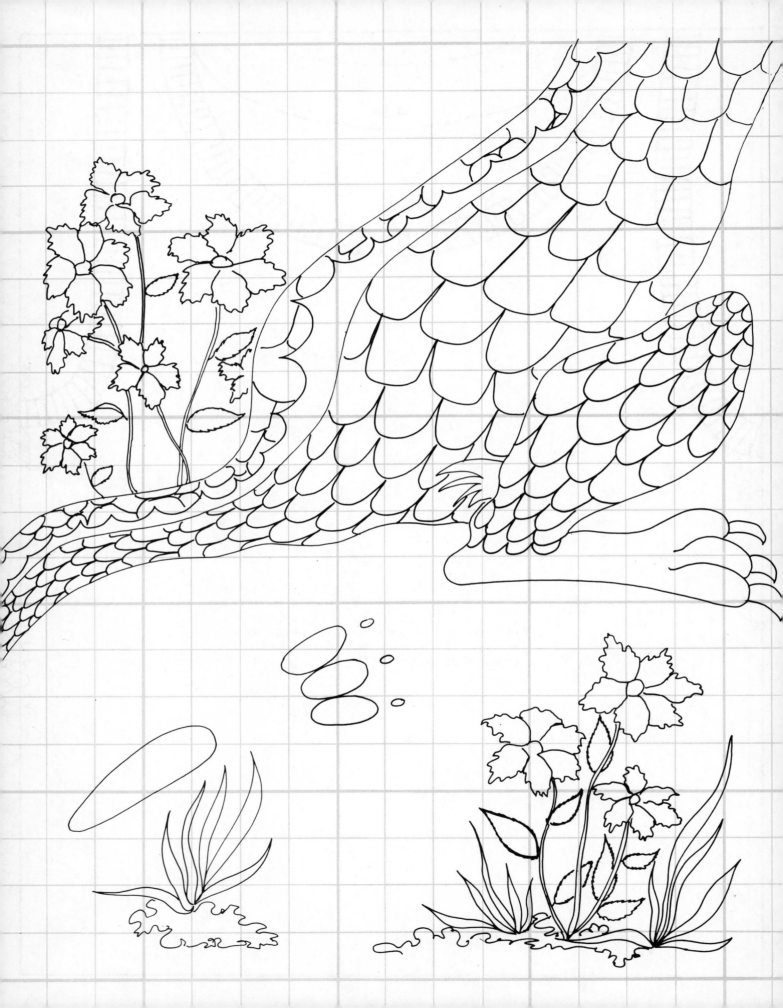

The illustrations on page 127 will show you how to place this dragon so he crawls all over the shirt.

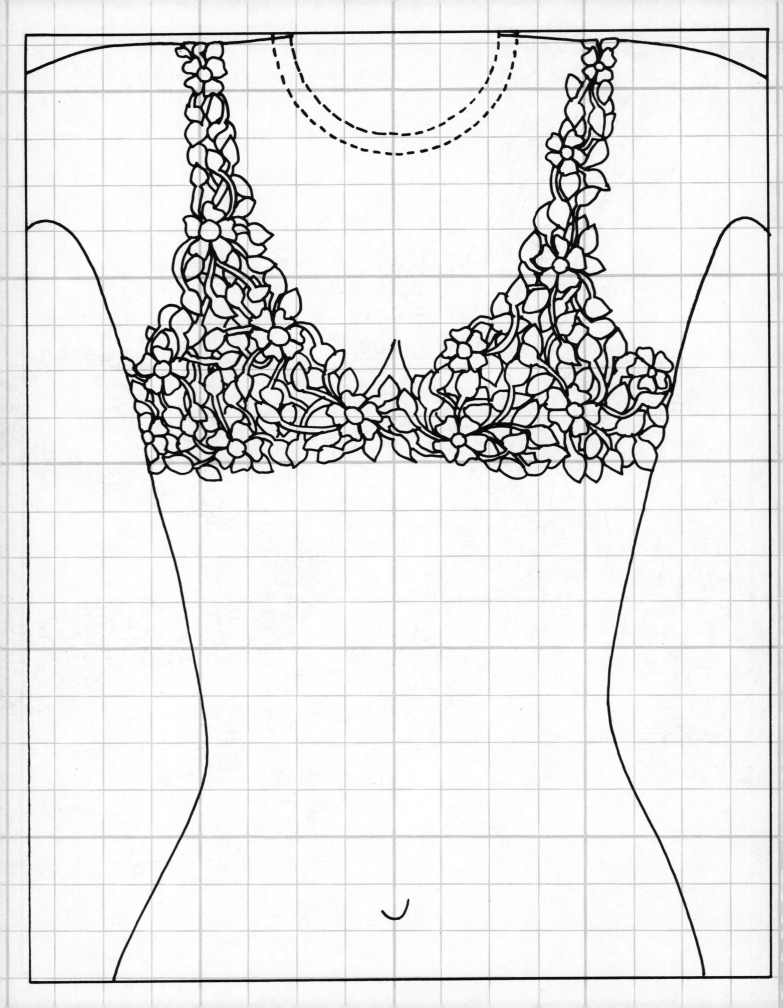

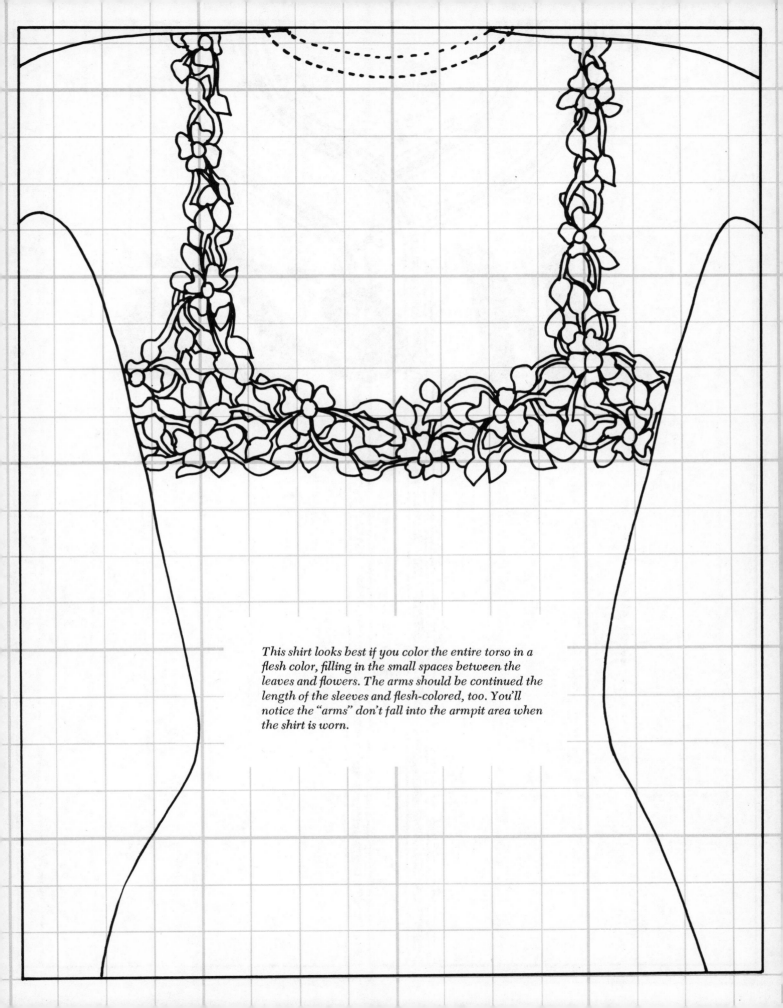

This shirt looks best if you color the entire torso in a flesh color, filling in the small spaces between the leaves and flowers. The arms should be continued the length of the sleeves and flesh-colored, too. You'll notice the "arms" don't fall into the armpit area when the shirt is worn.

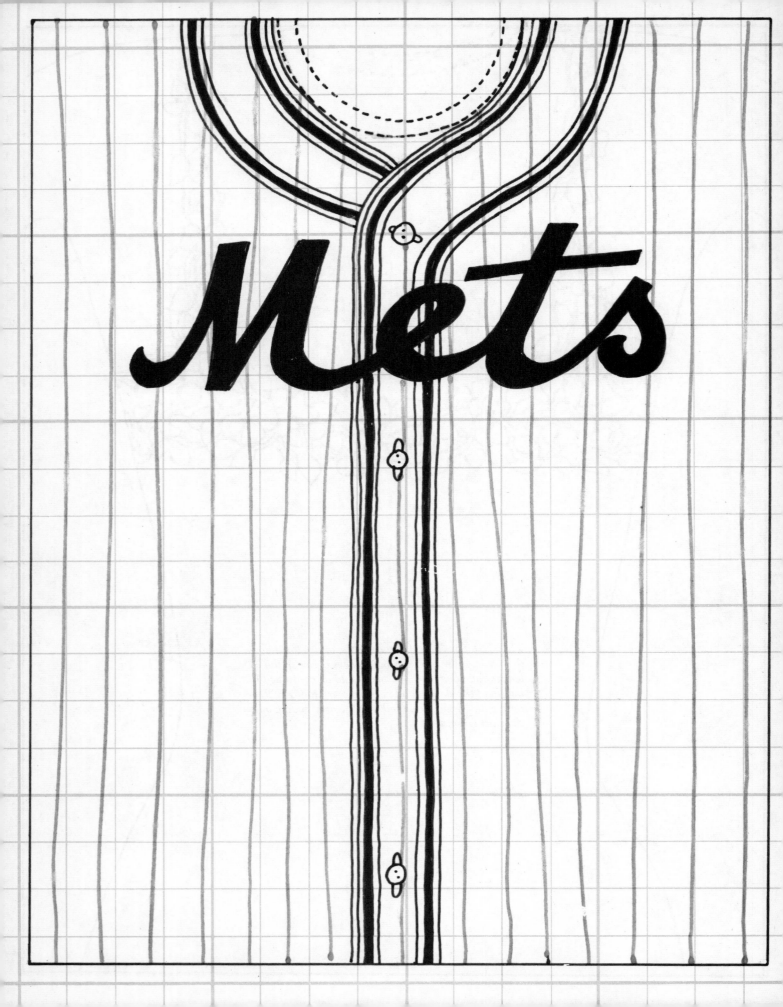

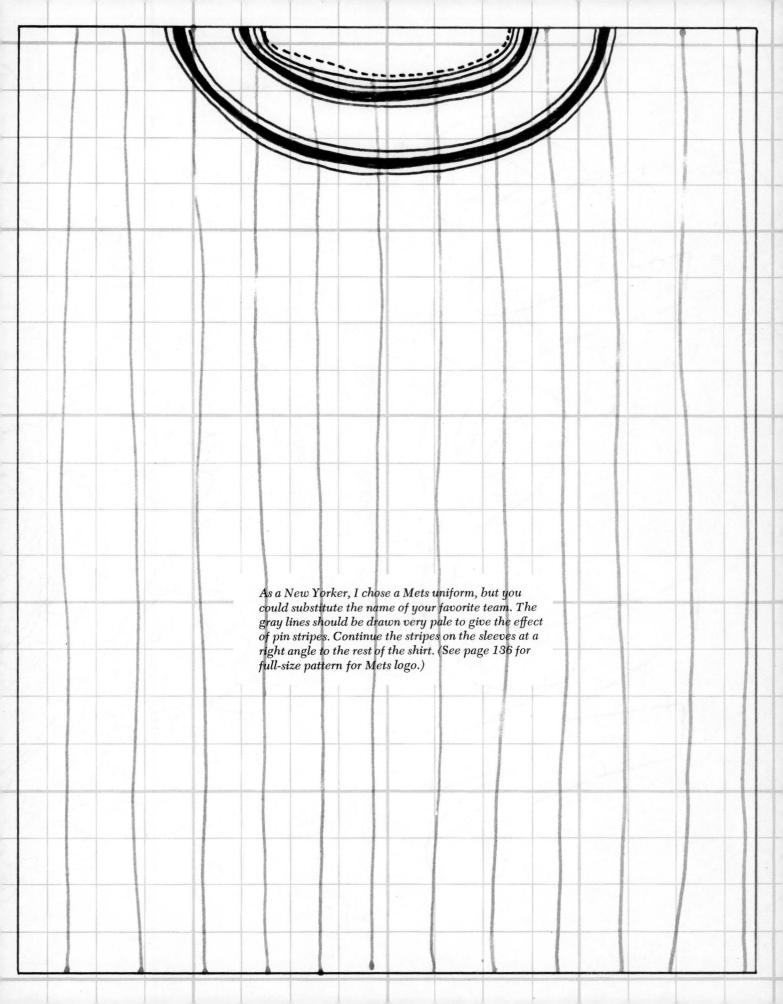

As a New Yorker, I chose a Mets uniform, but you could substitute the name of your favorite team. The gray lines should be drawn very pale to give the effect of pin stripes. Continue the stripes on the sleeves at a right angle to the rest of the shirt. (See page 136 for full-size pattern for Mets logo.)

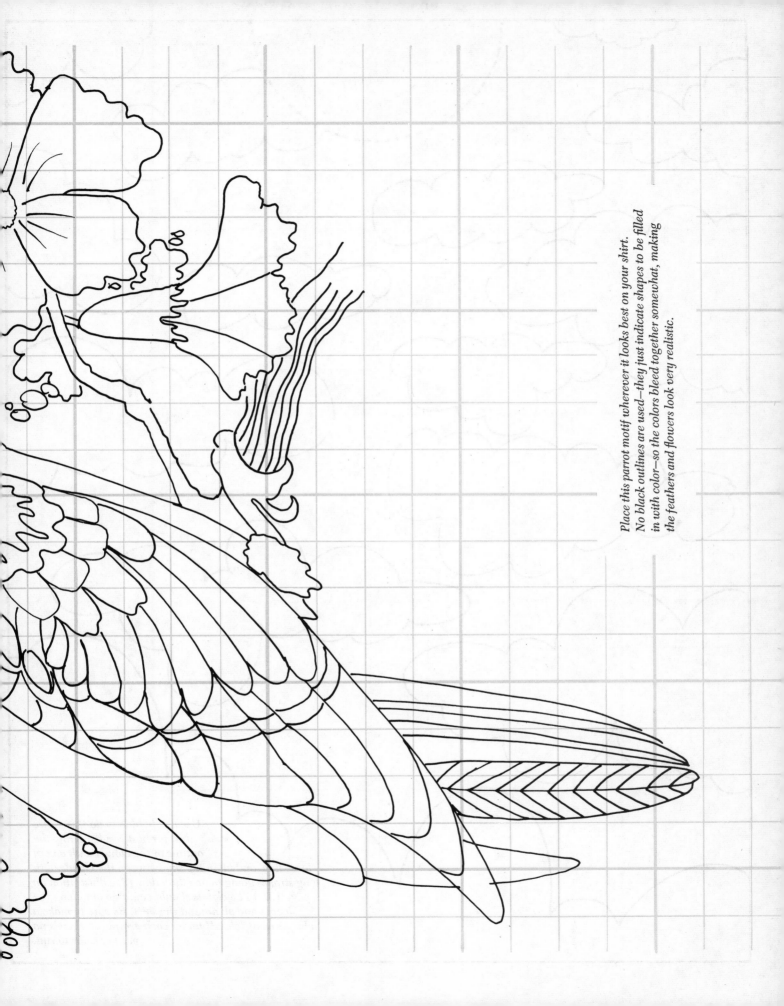

Place this parrot motif wherever it looks best on your shirt. No black outlines are used—they just indicate shapes to be filled in with color—so the colors bleed together somewhat, making the feathers and flowers look very realistic.

Use a pale blue to do this entire shirt for best results. Draw the outline of the clouds with a very loose line, and fill in the sky between the clouds with long strokes going in one direction. (See illustration on page 127.) The clouds should continue out along the sleeves and all around the shirt. Be sure to make a white area of "cloud" under each armpit, so there's no marker color to run.

Ties

*Shown in color on
pages 14 and 15*

A tie is the classic gift for a man, right? Well, why not a markered tie? Ties provide a ready-made surface, and ties in plain colors are inexpensive and come in many colors and fabrics. When buying a tie to marker, keep in mind the kind of design you want. If a hard, crisp line is what you're after, choose a pure cotton or wool, in a tight, non-bleeding weave. If you want a softer look, choose from the many synthetic blends.

No special tricks are involved when markering a tie, but don't carry the design too high or it will get lost in the knot. And remember, ties make especially good commemorative gifts —for birthdays, anniversaries, etcetera—and can easily be personalized with a name or monogram or an appropriate message.

Enlarge the pattern (whichever you decide on) to the correct size and transfer it by the carbon method. Most ties can be worked on as is; that is, they don't need to be stretched or taped to a work surface. Do put a piece of paper or cardboard between the layers as you work to prevent bleeding.

The colors you choose should fit the color of the tie you're markering, and the mood you want to achieve. The "Palm Beach" tie was meant to look a bit garish, so bright yellow, orange and green were just right. The one with the geometric design was supposed to look a bit more classy, so shades of blue, green and violet, close to the background color, were used. The city-scape tie is very subdued with the black, the grays and the browns. I was planning to color in the eagle tie until I saw that the fine-line marker I used bled so beautifully I decided to leave it as it was.

[139]

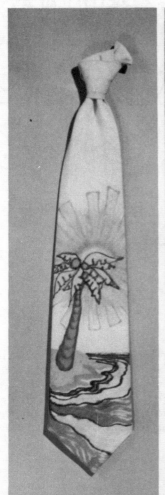

(Above): I drew this eagle tie with a fine black marker, intending to color it in, but the synthetic fabric gave such a nice, fuzzy bleed that I decided to leave it at that. (At right): Here is a take-off on the famous (notorious) Palm Beach tie—palm tree and clear, warm waters on a sunshiny yellow background.

(Above): This cityscape seemed the perfect subject matter for a gray tie. (At right): The tie only cost $1.50, but the geometric print makes it look like an expensive designer fabric.

Feather Fedora

This yellow fedora has a very simple design, and is perfect for anyone who wants to wear a feather in their cap.

Markering on a soft hat is a bit tricky. The brim is easy enough to work on, since it will lie flat on your work surface and can be turned as needed. To marker the crown, you'll need to stuff it with newspaper, or put it on a wig stand, or over a volleyball or any improvised mold.

If you feel that you actually need to trace the design, the hat can be temporarily flattened down and the design transferred using the carbon method. The simplest thing is just to lightly pencil a line to indicate the top and bottom line of the "hatband," using a tape measure to help give a straight line, and lightly copy the outline shapes of the buckle and feather. Be sure the buckle and feather are correctly placed at one side, with the feather going toward the back of the head.

The design for the brim is just a band of three stripes on the top and on the underside at the edge of the brim. Again, I recommend drawing these by hand, just staying at as even a distance as possible from the previously drawn line or from the edge. Alternatively, you can rough in the lines with a pencil, or you can mark dots ⅛″ (3 mm.), ½″ (1.25 cm.) and ⅛″ at intervals around the brim, and then connect the dots.

When coloring, remember that the colors may have a tendency to darken somewhat. On the hatband, I tried to simulate the look of grosgrain ribbon with the close vertical black lines, and by coloring each "rib" alternately with two similar colors.

Shown in color on page 14

Felt hats are fun to marker. Most dime stores sell them in a variety of styles and colors. It's easy to draw on felt, because the material gives a bit of resistance as you draw. On this inexpensive quality felt, the marker colors tended to darken a bit and the color took on a rather attractive chalky or crayony texture.

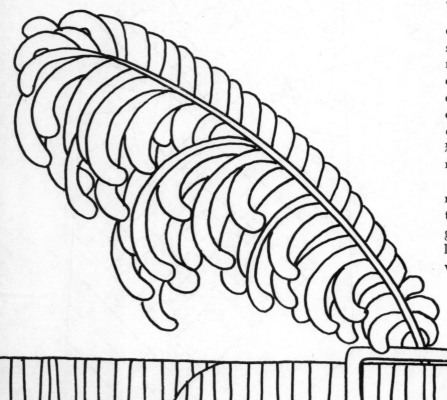

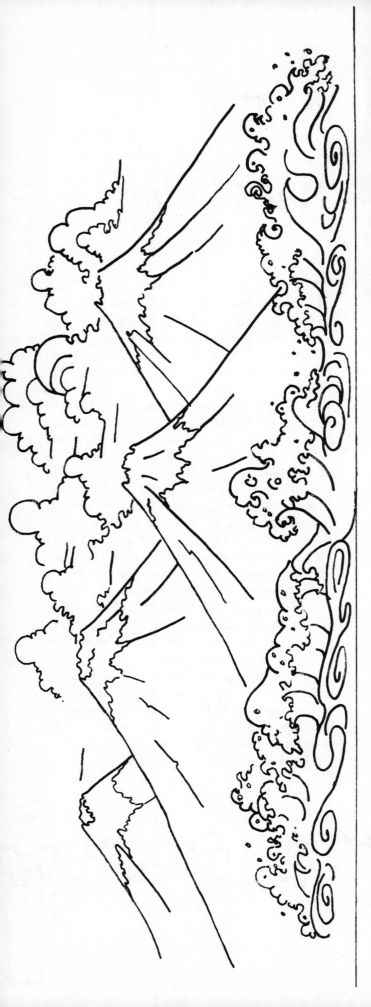

Shown in color on page 15

Japanese Felt Hat

The lovely pale blue of this felt hat inspired some experimentation with mixing the palest green, yellow and blue hues of marker to achieve shadows and variety in the mountains and waves. The mountains and waves were inspired by a Japanese woodblock print.

Mountains, clouds and waves are easy to do on a circular project such as this hat because it is not necessary to measure when using these design elements. Place three or four mountains of varying height at strategic locations on the hat and then slowly add the sea, more mountains, in front and behind the initial three or four, and clouds until you achieve the degree of sparsity or clutteredness that pleases you. You can also transfer the design by the carbon method.

The use of fine-line markers further emphasizes the delicacy of the design. Almost the entire hat is done with fine-line markers in shades of blue and green, some lighter and some darker than the pale blue of the hat itself. A few solid areas in the mountains and sky were colored in very pale markers.

Shown in color on page 15

Pink Cloche

This pink cloche is another dime-store purchase. The pattern is very simple—a row of interlocking flowers and leaves on the part of the brim that turns up, and one large flower off slightly to one side on the crown. Very sweet, feminine and springy.

To do the flower on the crown, try your hat on and decide where you want to place it, then make a pencil mark where the center will fall. If you're going to transfer the pattern in the book, make your tracing-paper copy and you can hold it up to the hat while you try it on to help you decide. You can flatten the hat for as long as it takes to transfer the design, but try not to crush it too much. Transfer the pattern by the carbon method. When drawing and coloring on the crown, do so over a mold of some sort as described in Feather Fedora on page 142. Leave the inside details of the flower—the veins on the leaves and petals, and the dots in the center, until after you color, to prevent blurring.

The brim is simpler because you can lay it flat on your work surface. Remember to work on the underside so that the flowers show when you turn it up. To draw the brim pattern, make pencil marks for the center of each flower 2″ (5 cm.) apart, ½″ (1.25 cm.) in from the edge of

the brim; you don't have to continue the pattern all around as it will not show in the back. Draw the flowers, then draw the single leaf going to the left from the underside of each flower, and finally the two leaves going to the right from the top of each flower (since these are overlapped by the single leaf, they must be drawn last).

The centers of the flowers on this hat are a bright magenta, the leaves a soft, mossy green, and the flowers a pink just a shade darker than the hat itself.

Shown in color on page 14

Straw Safari Hat

African motifs, loosely borrowed from *African Designs from Traditional Sources* by Geoffrey Williams (Dover Publications, Inc., New York, 1971), turn a plain straw hat into a Safari Special.

A pattern of three squares, which is repeated all the way around the brim, is given here. The design on the crown is placed at quarterly intervals, with a mask at the front and at the back, and crocodile motifs at each side. Transfer the patterns by the carbon method.

Our hat was done in earthy browns and blacks on the natural-colored straw, but it would also look nice in the bright reds, yellows, blues and blacks that we associate with African art.

[146]

A-Line Skirt

This blue cotton and polyester skirt cost only $3.99, but with the dark green marker motif it looks like an expensive designer fabric skirt. Any simple, uncluttered A-line dress or skirt could work with this pattern. It is easier to do than it looks (I did it entirely freehand) if you check the illustration as you read the instructions.

Tack or tape the skirt to your work surface at the top and side seams so that you can work on at least the top half of the front of the skirt. Place a sheet of newspaper or cardboard between the front and back of the skirt to prevent the marker from bleeding through as you work.

Shown in color on page 14

Measure the front of the skirt at the waistband and divide it so that you have an *uneven* number of scallops that will fit across the top row (this skirt has nine). If there is no center front seam on your garment, lightly pencil-mark a center line down the front as a guide. Mark another line about 1¾″ (4.5 cm.) below the waistband to indicate the depth of the first row of scallops. Starting at the center front and going out to the sides, marker the first row of scallops, so that you end up with a half-scallop at each side. Use a wide-tip marker angled to the side to get a somewhat thinner line than the flat tip would give you, but take advantage of the bleed to achieve a soft effect.

Make a line about 1¼″ (3 cm.) below the first row for the next (and each subsequent) row of scallops. Each scallop now starts at the bottom center of a scallop in the row above and connects to bottom center of the one next to it. Eliminating one scallop in each row, continue the rows of scallops until there is just one scallop straddling the center front seam. (See illustration.)

Draw the double line inside each scallop, and then add the center dot.

Move the skirt up on your work surface and re-tack it so that you can work from the hem up to the fourth row from the bottom of the scallop pattern.

Using a yardstick to guide you, draw a line from the juncture of the fourth and fifth scallop from the bottom out to the left side seam at the very bottom of the skirt. Draw four more parallel lines, from the junctures of each of the scallops below, and from the center of the bottom scallop (again, see illustration). Repeat on the other side.

Starting at the hem of the center front seam, draw a line at right angles to the lines just drawn, out to the outside line on the left side. Use a T-square or any square object to be sure you're getting a right angle. Repeat on the other side.

Using this line as your guide, draw lines parallel to it down to the hem of the skirt, far enough apart so that you create squares with the lines drawn. Repeat on the other side.

Draw horizontal lines to divide each of the squares you've just created and fill in the top half of each square.

Do the final embellishments: the rows of dots parallel to each of the diagonal lines, the freehand lines to make squares within the center square, and the flower in the middle.

To do the back of the skirt, turn it over, re-tack it so you can work on the top half, and place paper between the layers. Repeat the design on the back. In doing the first row, be sure to connect up the half-scallop on each side of the front with the half-scallop on each side of the back.

We did the entire skirt in one color—dark green marker on the medium blue skirt material. If you do your whole skirt in one color, choose it carefully to go with the background color. Of course, a multicolor scheme would also look nice—dark green with red and pink on a white or pink skirt, for example.

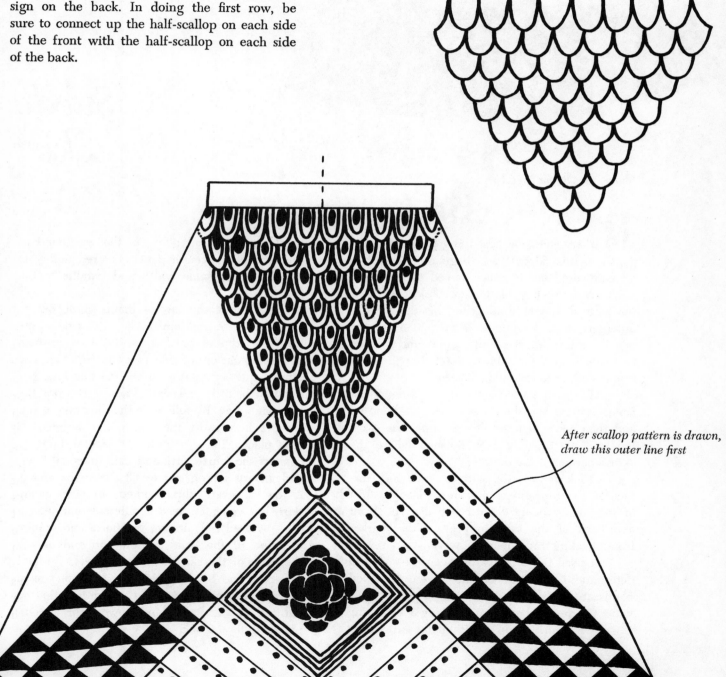

After scallop pattern is drawn, draw this outer line first

Shown in color on page 15

Suede Skirt

Markers were the best thing that ever happened to this skirt. It was beginning to look a bit careworn, and it *never* looked this good.

The structure of this gored skirt dictated the pattern. If you're adapting this design to a different skirt, I suggest that you rule (in pencil) a line for the center front and for the two side panels (see illustration). It will make it much easier to follow the design.

The skirt I used actually snaps down the front; I drew the design with the skirt closed and then continued the design under the overlap so that it would look finished where the skirt separates at the bottom.

Tack or tape the skirt to your work surface at the top and side seams. Place a sheet of newspaper or cardboard between the front and back of the skirt to prevent the marker from bleeding through as you work.

I used the distance between the snaps to determine the width of the seven V-shaped bands at the top; they are each 1½″ (3.75 cm.) wide. Do the top band first, forming a V starting 1½″ down from the top center of the skirt below the waistband, and going to the waistband at the sides of the center panel. The remaining six bands are the same width and parallel to the first.

To start the row of bands going out to the sides at the bottom of the skirt, rule a line from the edge of the last band out to the hem of the skirt at either side (see illustration). The other bands again run parallel to this line, but the fourth, fifth and sixth lines start from the side panel line. By following the illustration, you can see how easily the rest of the design falls into place: Three parallel horizontal lines to connect the fourth, fifth and sixth diagonal lines, and a fiery setting sun to fill the space above. A row of seven tulips worked out best on my skirt, but you may need a different number.

I used red, brown, turquoise and orange to color all the bands at the top and out to the sides of the skirt. For the flowers, I added red, pink and bright green. But you don't have to color everything in; you could just do the outlines of the bands and flowers for a completely different look.

[150]

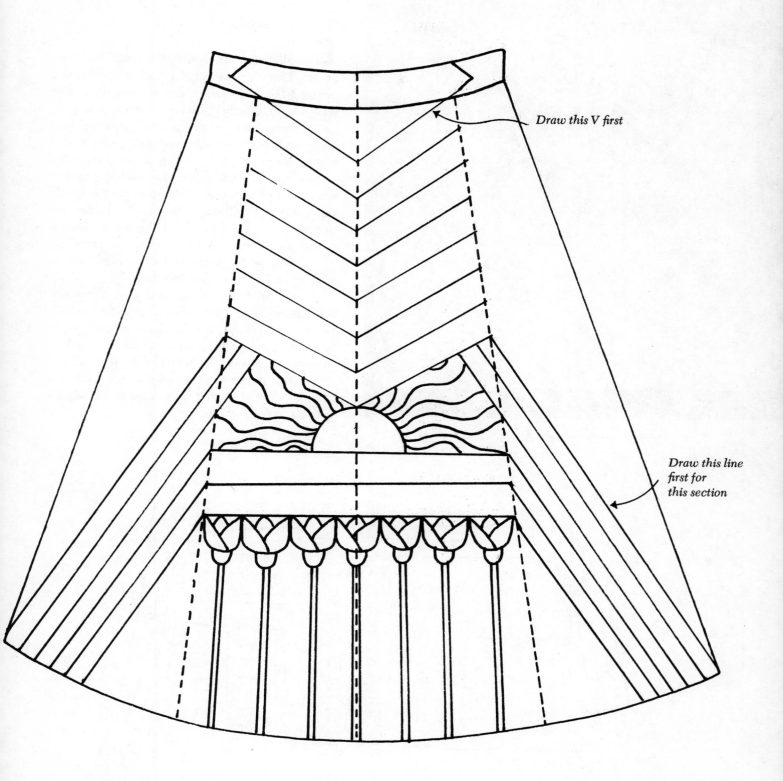

Draw this V first

*Draw this line
first for
this section*

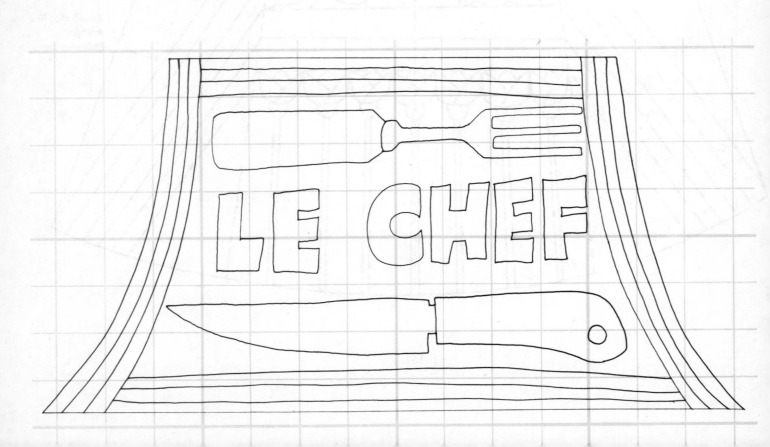

Barbecue Apron

Compliment your chef with his own barbecue apron. The big semicircular pocket on this one inspired the watermelon design, and it's a nice watermelon, whether it fits on a pocket or not.

Since your work surface probably isn't large enough to enable you to work on the whole apron at once, stretch it on your work surface with a little newspaper padding underneath so that you can work either on the whole top section (Le Chef) or the whole middle section at once. Then just shift the apron around on the work surface to move to the other area.

Enlarge the patterns and transfer them to your apron by the carbon method.

When doing the main design, draw just the outline of the watermelon and the seeds in black. For the rest, overlap hues of dark green to light green to near white to pink to red as you work in toward the center of the melon.

You might want to substitute a name for the "Le Chef" lettering. If so consult the alphabets on pages 194-200.

Shown in color on page 14

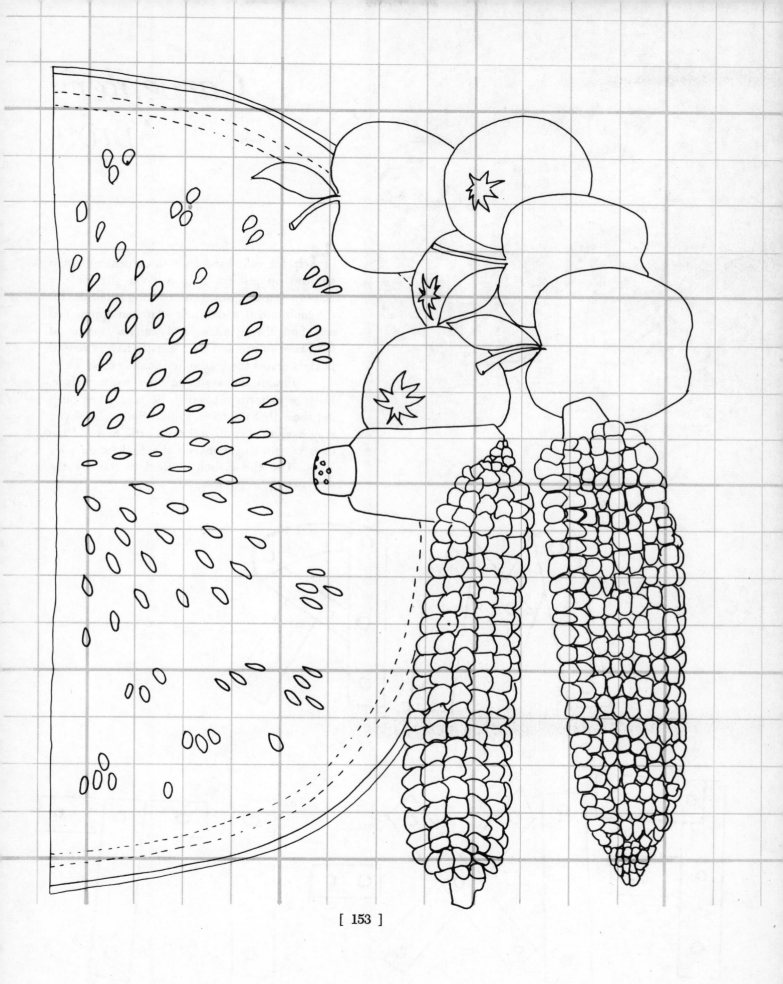

Carpenter's Apron

Help for your handyman—a carpenter's apron spruced up just for him. A good gift for any helping hand. Substitute cooking utensils for the tools and it makes a fine kitchen apron. You can find these unbleached canvas aprons at hardware stores, and they usually have a row of pockets across the bottom for holding tools.

Fasten the apron to your work surface. Enlarge patterns if needed. Be sure when placing them that the tools go into the pockets—you may have to rearrange them a little to avoid the lines of stitching between the pockets on your apron. Use the carbon method to transfer the design.

Shown in color on page 15

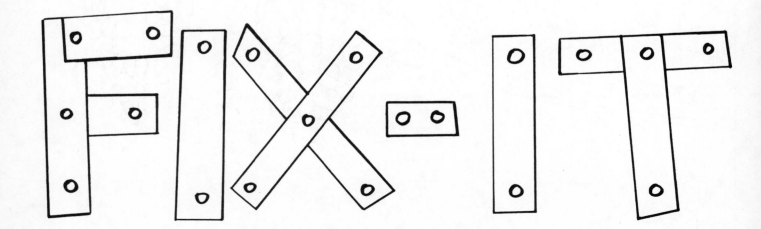

The next step is to make each individual pocket look like the end of a crate. A pattern is given here for the pockets; you may have to adjust the size. First draw the four slats that form the border, giving them a three-dimensional look as shown in the pattern. Then draw the diagonal cross pieces inside the border. Place "screw" heads at corners and strategic places. Then transfer the rest of the pattern, again adjusting where necessary. If, however,

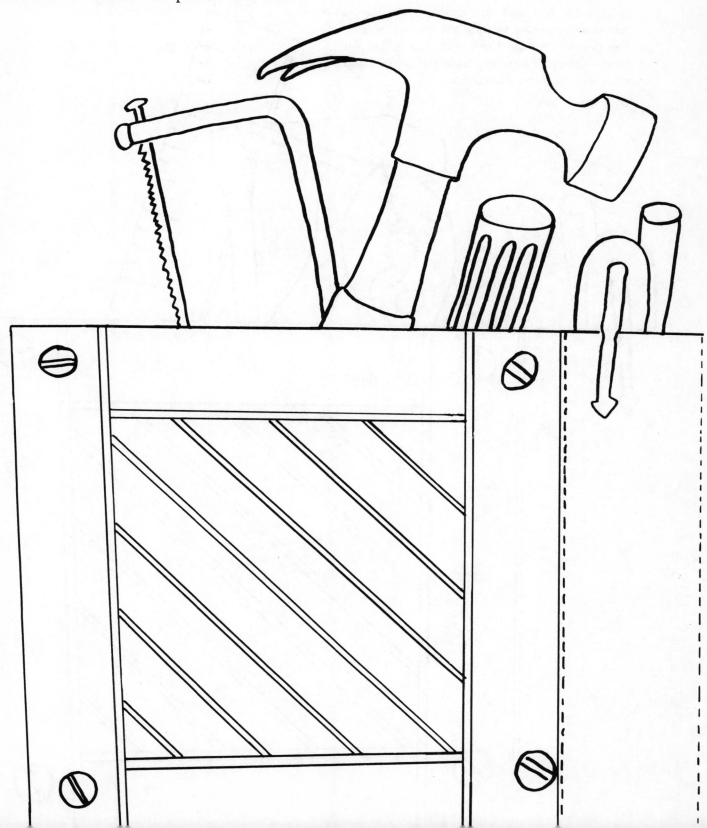

the enlarged patterns are the same size as your pockets, simply trace and transfer the whole design.

Reposition the apron on the work surface to do the "Mr. Fix-it" motif at the top. Transfer the pattern by the carbon method. The idea is to achieve a look of random wood pieces hammered together to form the letters, so color the design to look like wood and nails. Put cardboard or newspaper inside the pockets and under the apron for protection.

As usual, when the design is supposed to "fool the eye," I color it as realistically as possible—the pockets are done in wood colors, and the tools in metallic-looking grays. But more fanciful colors would look just fine.

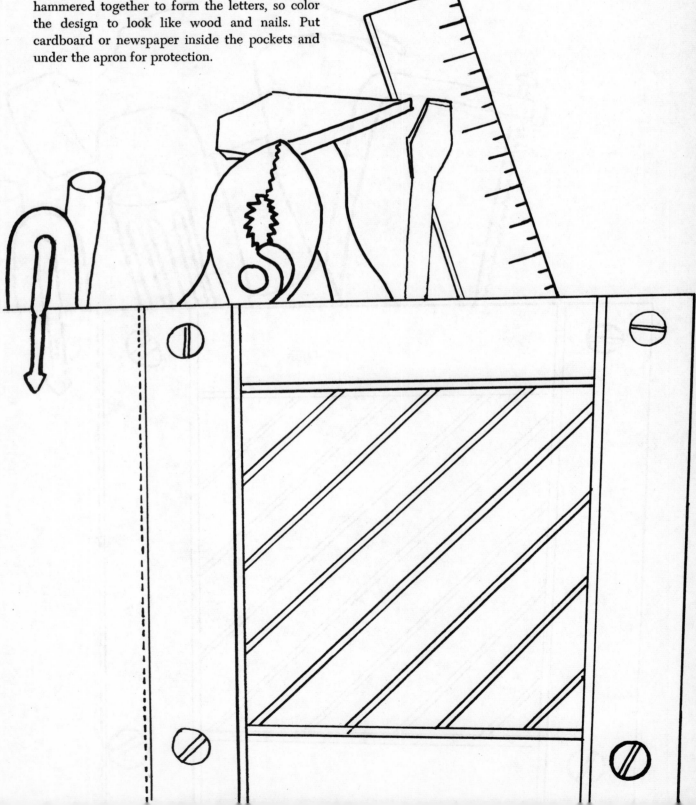

Shown in color on page 14

Hostess Apron

One of the nicest things about using markers is that they're so quick—you can make a festive hostess apron like this in an hour, so that even if you only wear it for a few weeks during the holidays, you get ample enough reward for your efforts.

The pattern can be transferred using the carbon method, after enlarging it to the proper size. Tack the apron to your work surface, stretching it taut. Have some paper padding under the apron for protection and support. The pattern of bells should be pretty well centered on the apron. The holly, bells, stars and candy canes can be placed on the apron wherever they look best.

The usual Christmas colors—red and green—with a little blue and yellow make up the color scheme.

[157]

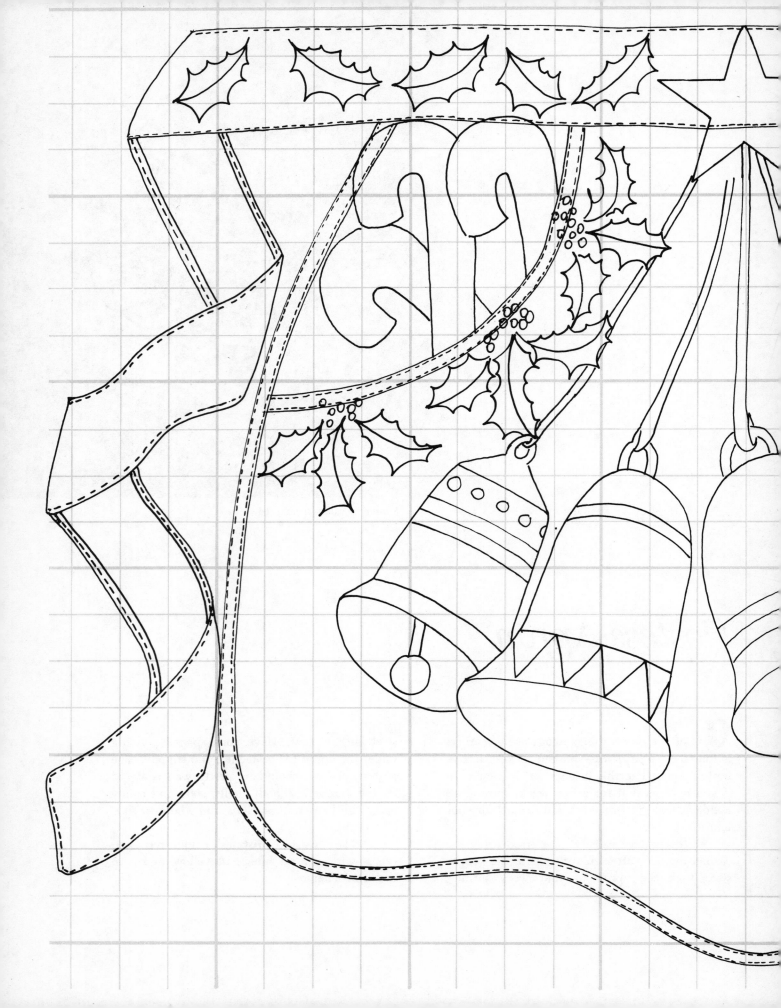

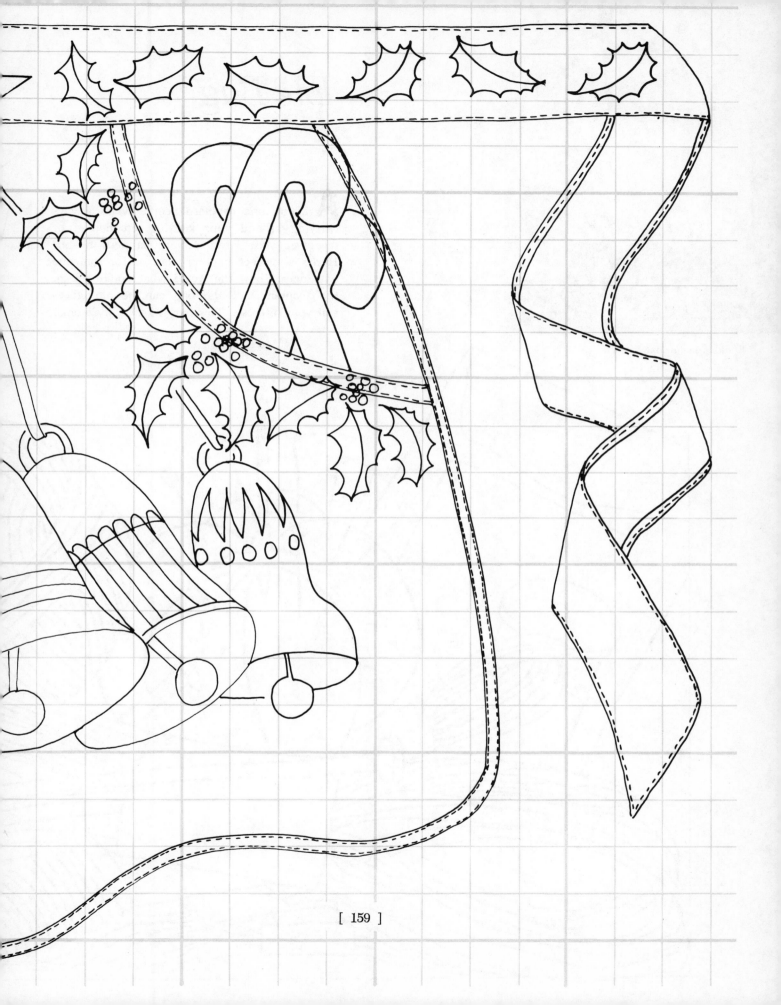

Tote Bag

Shown in color on page 15

Are you one of those people who's always carrying around your knitting, crocheting, or whatever your latest project happens to be? Here's a perfect bag for you, or for someone who does. Show the world what you're up to; the "contents" of the bag can be altered to suit your interests. This bag is 14½" (36.25 cm.)

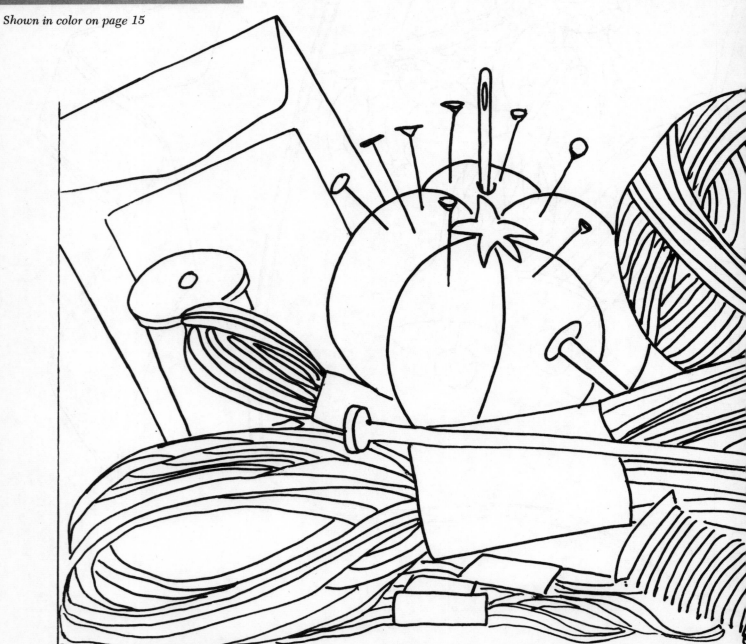

square. If your bag is a different size, adjust the pattern as needed.

Enlarge the pattern to the size you need and transfer it to your bag using the carbon method. Just lay the bag flat on your work surface, but be sure to place a piece of paper or cardboard between the layers to prevent bleeding.

Color the things in the bag as realistically as possible for the best effect, using bright markers for the yarn and thread to give life to the color scheme.

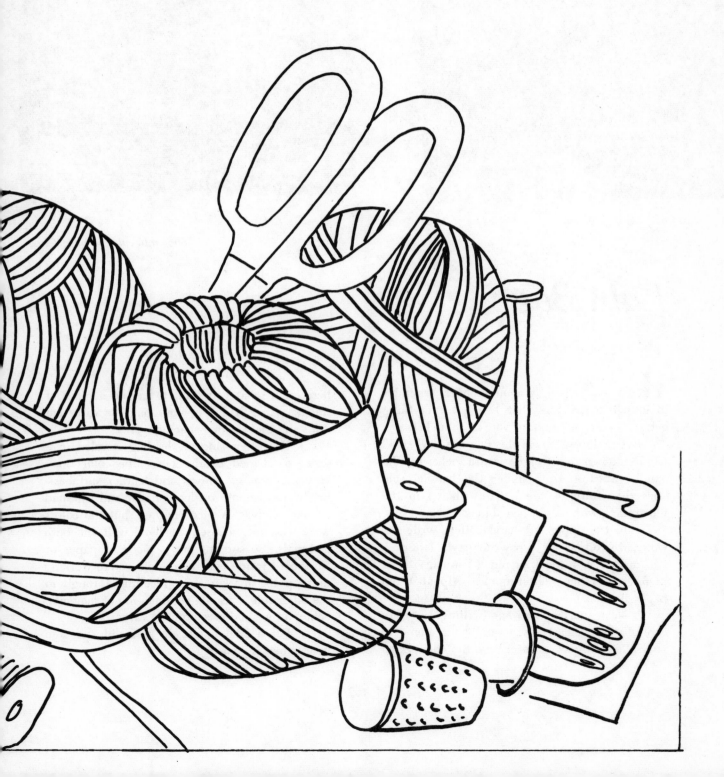

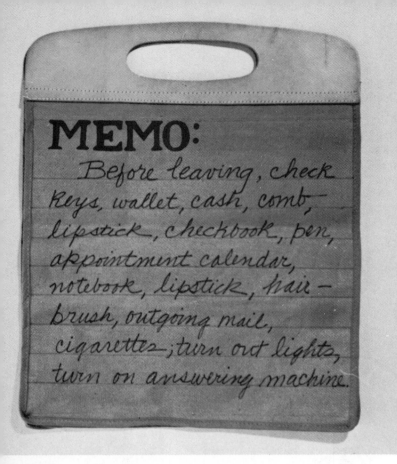

Shown in color on page 14

Lulu Bag

Here's *my* bag, a tongue-in-cheek reminder to myself to be sure that I've got everything before leaving my studio—you do your list.

The dimensions of this bag are 13½″ x 14″ (33.75 x 35 cm.) with a few extra inches for the handle. Starting from under the handle, rule lines the width of the bag, as shown in the illustration, with a light pencil line.

In the upper left hand corner, write the word MEMO: in its typewriter style lettering, and marker it in black or red. (You can, if you prefer, use fancier lettering. See Alphabets on pages 194-200.)

Next, in your own handwriting, but very carefully and clearly, write out your memo to yourself. If you want to change the copy given

here, plan what you want to say on a piece of tracing paper laid over your bag. Be sure that it fits and that the line-spacing works.

The other side of the bag is ruled in a series of striped bands. The same colors look very different on canvas and leather surfaces—bright and smooth on leather, flat and subdued on dark canvas. A nice contrast, but the colors were carefully chosen to look well on both materials. Be sure to put a piece of paper or cardboard inside your bag while you're working to keep the marker from bleeding through to the other side. I used a combination of magenta, ochre, brown and green for the stripes.

For a final touch, do as I did and sign your name on your bag.

[162]

MEMO:

Before leaving, check keys, wallet, cash, comb, lipstick, checkbook, pen, appointment calendar, notebook, compact, hair-brush, outgoing mail, cigarettes, turn out lights, turn on answering machine.

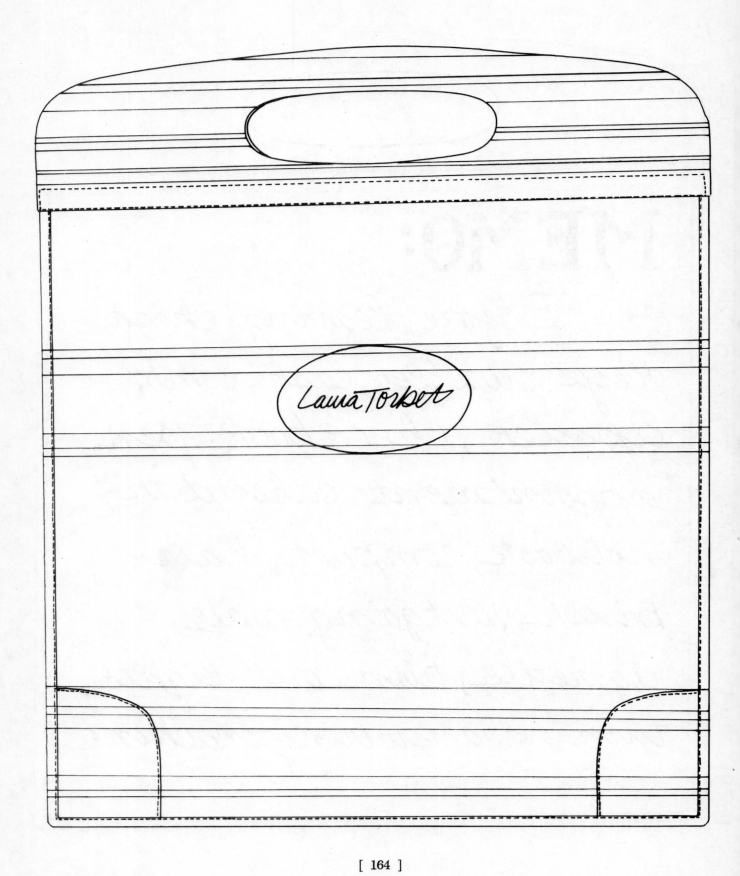

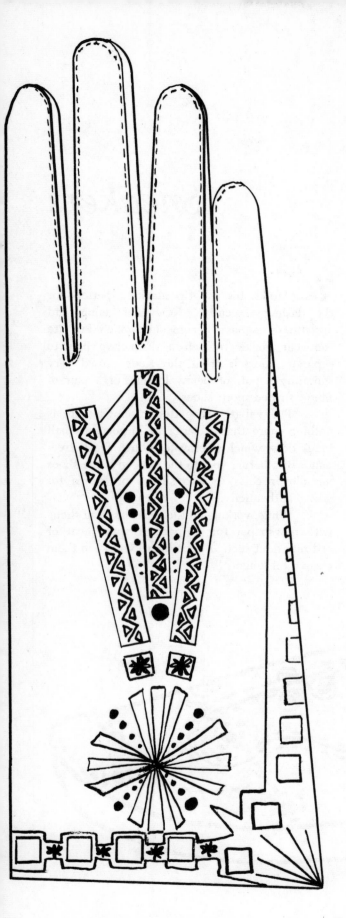

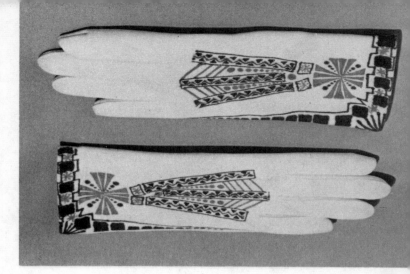

Shown in color on page 15

Gloves

Geometric patterning makes these white gloves something special, and they're very easy to work on. The soft cotton takes quite a fine marker line. There are many motifs which would be nice on gloves. You could steal an idea from the print or pattern of a favorite dress or suit. Try rings and bracelets or anything else you like or have a fancy for. Cross your palms with silver; or wear your heart in your hands.

When you work on gloves, a piece of cardboard cut to the width of the palm of the glove, helps to hold the glove taut as you work and to keep the marker from bleeding through to the other side.

The pattern shown here can be transferred to the glove using the carbon method. The design should be placed on the back of the glove, in the center. The detail in the design is quite small; if you have them, use templates to help with the tiny geometric shapes (see Tools and Tips on page 23).

Red and blue were the basic colors used for our gloves. The color of your own coat or dress should dictate the colors you use.

Shown in color on page 15

Sneakers

Yessir, folks, it's wingtip sneakers—perfect for the dashing executive. Now that tennis and athletic shoes have become everyone's favorite footwear, make yourself a distinctive pair to separate yourself from the Keds crowd. Try imitating a pair of penny loafers, or a pair of fancy, striped sports shoes.

The wingtip shoe design shown here is nothing more than a series of large and small black dots, which is easy to follow. Do it free-hand. But, before you do the dots, give the shoes an allover color in two shades of brown for added authenticity.

While working on the sneakers, stuff them with newspaper for support. A spray coat of soil retardant such as Scotchgard will keep them clean a bit longer.

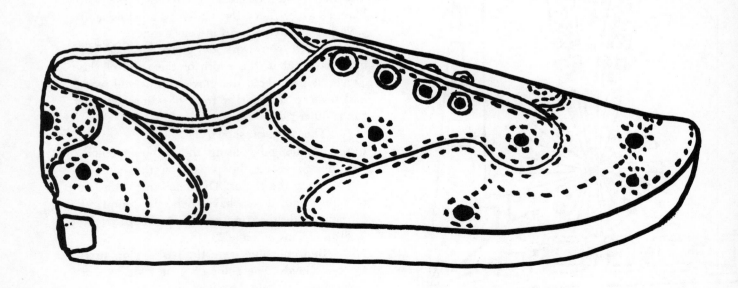

Espadrilles

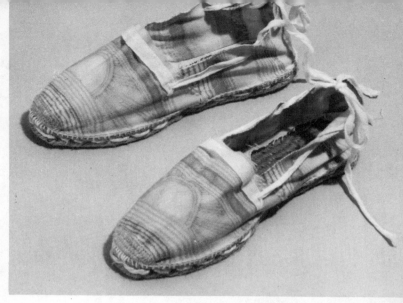

Shown in color on page 14

Canvas shoes in many styles and colors are very popular these days—espadrilles like those shown here are even available in dime stores. They look great markered. Markers can also rescue a pair of canvas shoes which have become stained or dingy with wear. They're easy to work on too, because the canvas weave makes it easy to draw straight lines.

You can see from the illustration that the design is very simple—random bands of wide and narrow lines in a chosen selection of colors and a sun motif on the front and back. Do the front section and center back first, and then fill in the sides with lines. Draw the design freehand.

I used a rather Mexican-looking combination of bright pink, yellow, turquoise and green,
all in fine-line markers with just a few areas between the bands filled in yellow. And the sun is done in solid yellow.

Stuff the espadrilles with newspaper to give you some support while you're working. When you're through, spray them with a soil retardant such as Scotchgard to protect the marker design from wear.

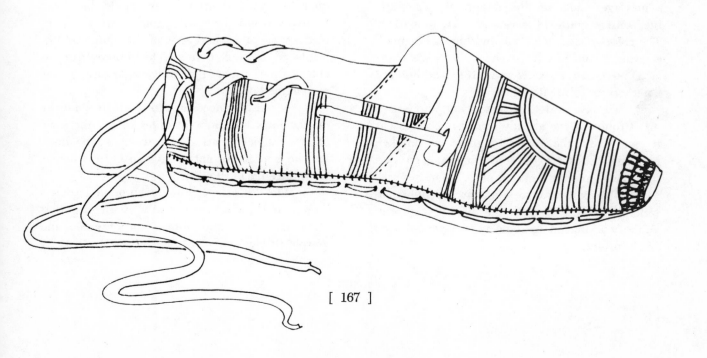

[167]

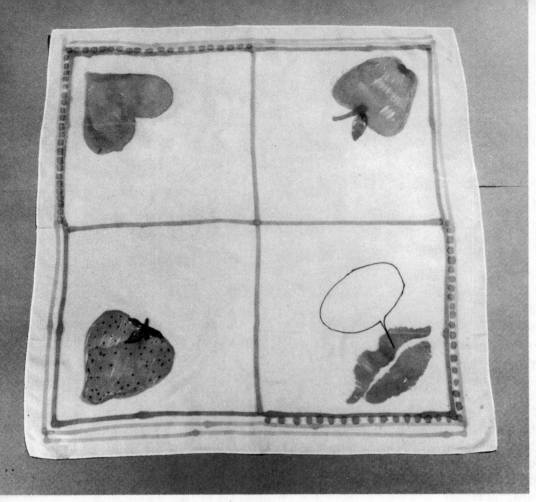

Scarf

Shown in color on page 14

Four simple motifs, all red—a strawberry, an apple, a heart, lips with a cartoon balloon for a message—make up the design of this scarf. Inexpensive synthetic scarves are easy to marker. The color goes on smoothly and bleeds like mad, creating beautiful effects where the colors overlap. Loose, casual motifs and a freehand line are a natural for this material.

To save a lot of measuring and marking, I followed the already ironed-in creases (as it came from the store) to guide my marker, breaking the scarf up into quarters. To personalize, sign your name in one corner.

The best way to work on this light material is to tape or tack the area of the scarf you're working on to some newspaper on your work surface.

The accompanying photograph shows you the basic layout of the scarf: it is divided in quarters; these division lines should be done as two crossed lines with dots, with a border of the same all around. One of the design motifs is placed in each corner. The designs can be enlarged as usual and transferred, using the carbon method.

It's almost necessary to work freehand to do the lines and dots, in order to get the look of a "designer" scarf. Don't worry if the lines for the border are not always an even distance from the edge of the scarf.

On the pale yellow background I used a bright red almost exclusively, with the dots done in brown, and with a bit of green and purple thrown in.

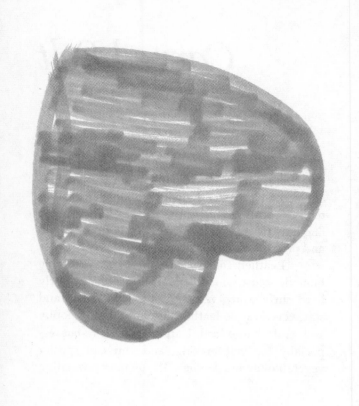

Tooled Belt

Carved Belt

Pre-stamped and tooled leather provides a ready-made pattern for markering—like having a coloring book. Leather wallets, purses and belts seem to be the most common tooled items available.

No special tricks here. Use fine-line markers for getting into the finely tooled crevasses—dark colors will give you the best definition. Just color the rest in; for the best results use colors that are not too dark to retain the maximum detail.

The background of the belt is a dark purple; the flowers are done in dark pink and red and the leaves in two shades of green. The result is a very traditional-looking pattern in very contemporary colors. The belt is finished with a light coat of Feibing's tan antique finish (see Markering on Leather and Suede, page 26).

The thin black lines on this plain leather belt are actually carved in with a linoleum-cutting tool. You can just copy the pattern with a black fine-line marker, but carving is both a simple and pretty technique, as you'll see.

Leather for carving must be vegetable tanned. Most smooth leathers with a fairly hard surface are vegetable tanned (suede and soft, very flexible leathers are not). Many hobby and craft stores sell leather strips pre-cut especially for belt making, and you can specify vegetable-tanned leather. If you're rejuvenating

Shown in color on page 14

Shown in color on page 15

an old belt, you'll have to test it with the linoleum cutter—the tool just won't work on any other kind of leather. Linoleum cutting tools can be found in any craft or hobby shop and in many dime stores. They come with a set of several interchangeable blades. For leather carving, use the one with the deep V-shaped blade.

Carving the leather is very simple; work just as you would in cutting a linoleum block. Draw your design with a light pencil line or transfer this pattern by the carbon method. Insert the blade gently where you want to begin a line, and simply push the blade along, away from you, maintaining a firm and even pressure. Stop the forward motion of the tool at the end of the line, and lift up, severing the sliver of leather which you will have extracted. More complete instructions, if you need them, come in the package when you purchase the linoleum cutter.

In carving this pattern, cut first the lines running along the top and bottom edges the length of the belt. Then you can start and finish all the other shorter lines in between, using these lines as your guide. Maintaining an absolutely straight line isn't essential (though you can use a ruler to guide you). Your hand is bound to wobble a bit and there will be a thick-to-thin quality to the line, which isn't bad at all.

To color, darken all the incised lines with a fine-line marker, and color in all other areas and the edges of the belt. To finish, see instructions for finishing leather under Markering on Leather and Suede, page 26; the antique finish described is perfect for tooled leather.

The colors we used were a very strong red, orange, blue and green, chosen so they will still be lively after given a coat of tan antique finish.

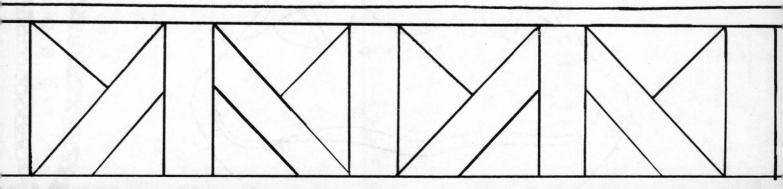

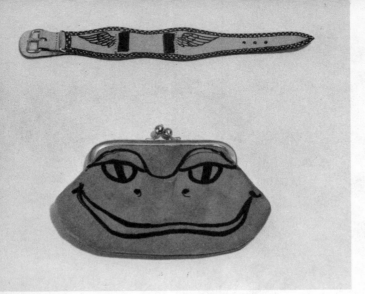

Watchband
and
Change Purse

Shown in color on page 14

With a little help from your markers, a plain leather watchband can look pretty snazzy. This one was done using just a black fine-line marker in a winged motif (time flies) with a small checkerboard border all around. Use a little bit of antique finish to seal the marker color and give the band a rich surface texture (see Markering on Leather and Suede, page 26).

Since your watchband is not likely to be exactly the same size and shape as the one shown here, it would be difficult to transfer the checkerboard border. But you get the idea—just do two rows of small squares all the way around your watchband. Use a pencil to do the preliminary drawing; the

marker will cover it. The pattern for the wings can be traced and transferred with the carbon method. Be sure to place it so that one of the wings is on each side of the watch itself.

A black fine-line marker was used to do this entire watchband; a more colorful version would also look nice.

Sometimes the shape of an object suggests what design should be on it. This small suede change purse was just looking for this big silly grinning face.

The design can be transferred using the carbon method. But the fun of this project is that the shape of the purse itself gives the grinning face its shape. Stuff the purse with paper first; you'll find it makes your work easier. A brown fine-line marker was used to draw the basic design, and a bit of color was added for the eyes and tongue.

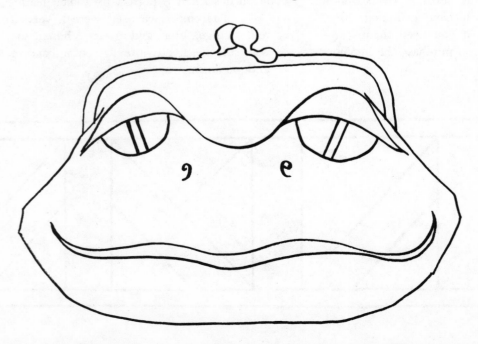

Tattoos

Here's a very silly idea, but it's one which my friends and I have had a lot of fun with. Decorate your body with tattoos. They're quick to do, the subject matter is endless, and they'll last a few days unless they come in contact with too much soap and water. Unless your skin is very sensitive, a small tattoo shouldn't be an irritant. It's fun to experiment with such impermanent tattoos, fun to wear them to the pool or beach. They can be scrubbed off with soap and water, or removed very easily with a bit of nail polish remover.

Be sure your skin is clean and dry when you apply the marker, or it will smear easily. It's a bit tricky to transfer the designs in the usual way—and it takes the fun out of it. Muster up your courage and test your drawing skills on yourself or your friend. And color as you please.

[173]

Shown in color on page 16

Child's Chair

This little chair is a beloved favorite of its proud owner, Jane, and it looks great in her room. Personalized, fanciful children's furniture and toys—chairs, desks, rocking horses, toy chests—are just the right size and just the right subjects for markering.

The seat of the chair is ruled in a bull's-eye pattern of red, yellow and green. Like the seat, the back of the chair has a border of two stripes and a place in the center for a name or monogram. All details of the chair—legs, edges, rungs, etcetera, carry through the striped pattern. You can use a tape measure or masking tape to guide the marker over these curved surfaces.

It's best if you draw the entire design first with a light pencil line. Determine the center of the seat of the chair, and, using a compass (see Tools and Tips, page 23), draw the bull's-eye in the center. Next, determine the position of the lines radiating out to the sides of the seat of the chair from the bull's-eye. Decide where you want to place the animals and transfer them to the chair using the carbon method.

We drew the outlines of the animals using fine-line markers, then colored in the background with wide-tip markers. Red, yellow, blue, orange and brown were used.

Be sure to seal the design with a coat of sealer such as Varathane.

Schoolbag

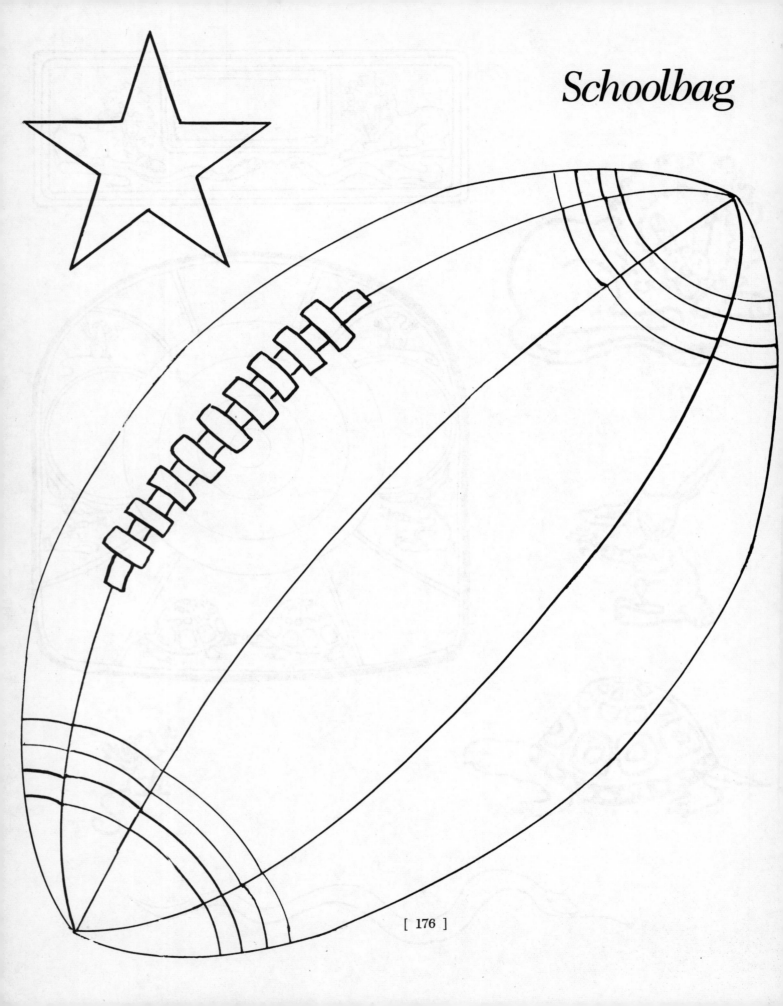

This ladies' shoulder bag, all $1.99 of it, makes a roomy, rah-rah schoolbag for a sports-minded boy. The motif would also look good on the front and back of a sweatshirt or T-shirt.

The design consists of a football on the front, an athletic letter on the back, and a pattern of stars and stripes on each side. You could also go all the way and marker all around the sides and along the strap. As for the letter, the initial of the school or the student will do. The letters are a very blocky style and not hard to draw yourself. Be sure to use your school colors for this project.

To facilitate working on the bag, stuff it full of newspapers (or whatever) to pad it out. To transfer the design, use the carbon method.

Use a soil retardant such as Scotchgard to seal in your handiwork.

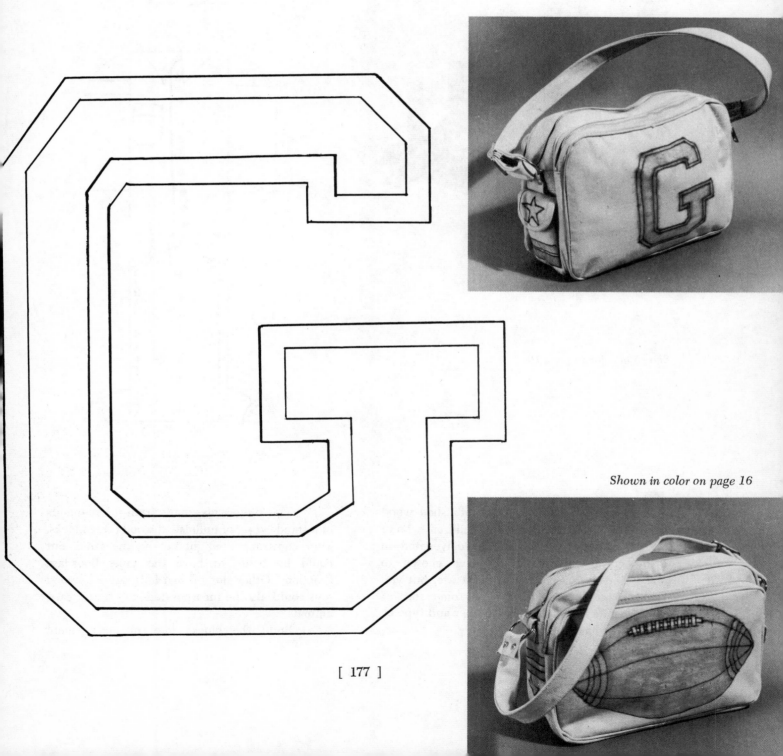

Shown in color on page 16

[177]

Shown in color on page 16

Blocks

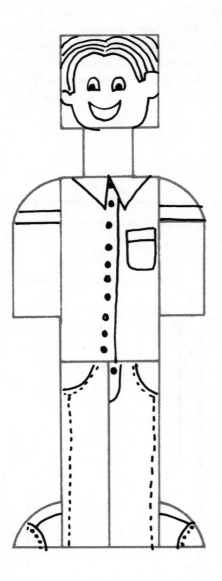

Do you have an old set of unfinished wood children's blocks around, and children who've outgrown them? They can be rejuvenated in many ways with markers. We've chosen to make them into a castle-cum-bookcase, but you could make a wall plaque or some sort of container, depending on the number and type of blocks you have.

This project was made from the remnants of a standard set of unfinished wood table blocks. Your construction might not be the same, but could be made to have the same bookcase function. Other long-discarded natural wood toys could also be incorporated—toy trains, cars, animals.

Build the blocks into an arrangement

which suits you. Decide on your color scheme. Color the blocks one at a time and return them to their place, keeping the arrangement intact. We used a bit of every color for this project, though we kept the color layout symmetrical. The basic colors are red, magenta, yellow and blue. On a project like this, the brighter the color, the better it looks.

You might want to add more detail with stripes, dots, doors, windows, even decals or transfer lettering. Finally, glue the arrangement together with a sturdy, fast-drying glue like Wil-Bond Cement, and spray with Varathane.

The accompanying illustrations show alternative ideas for recycling the blocks. Try the block people—a group of them would look nice mounted on a wall. Or, arrange the blocks in a solid mass as shown, and do a drawing on top and bottom. Don't glue the pieces together, and you've got two picture puzzles. You might even get your child or children to do the drawings and markering. It's the sort of thing children love to do.

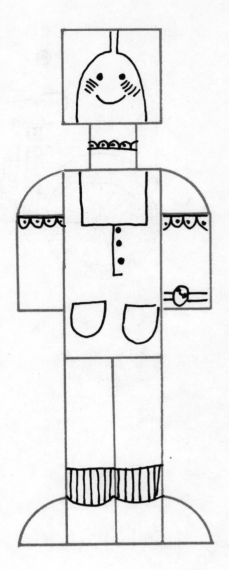

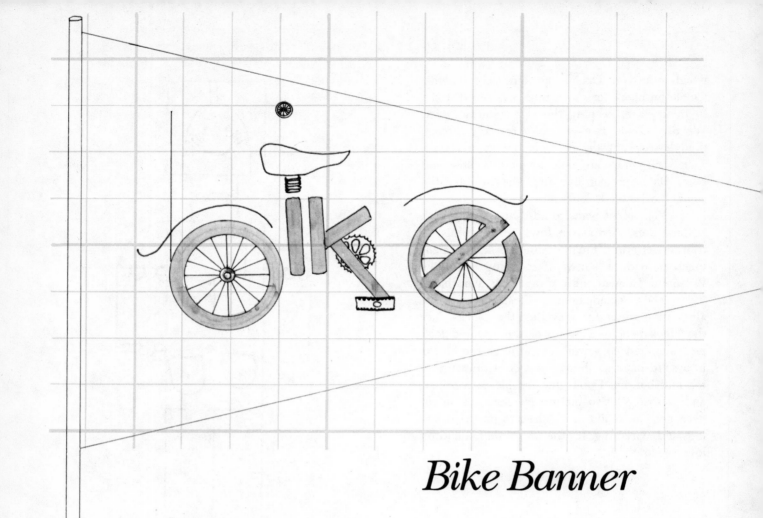

Bike Banner

Another good project for kids is pennants or bike banners, or just flags to fly from the walls of their room. Banners or flags can be cut from remnants of fabric in the size and shape you want. Turn the edges under and run a seam all the way around. If you plan to hang the flag on a rod or dowel, sew a wide hem at the side for the rod to slip through.

The pattern given here can be enlarged as usual and transferred using the carbon method. We just used a ruler and compass and did the rest freehand. To add interest to this design, you might add a border of stripes or polka dots all the way around.

Tack the fabric to the work surface to hold it in place, and put a newspaper under it for protection.

We used red, brown, gray and green on the shiny yellow background.

Shown in color on page 16

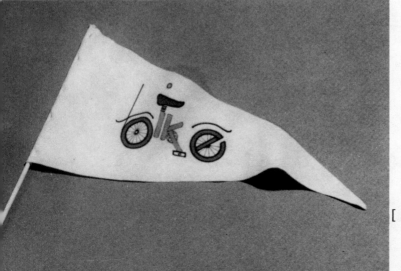

Plastic Bottles

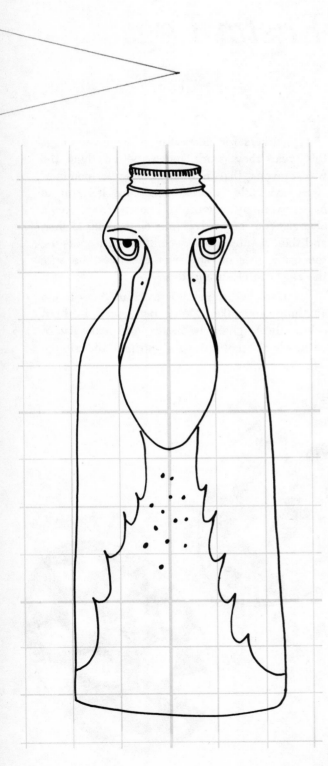

Plastic bottles and containers are ideal for children to marker. Children can make things for their own use, such as pencil containers, catch-all boxes, puppets, or they can make their own markered gifts. These bottles can be cut and shaped with a serrated knife or scissors, if you want to use them as containers. Any rough edges can be smoothed off with a bit of sandpaper.

The bottle shown here is meant just as an example of what you can do. These bottles come in many sizes and shapes.

My bottle somehow turned into a big yellow and gray bird with an orange beak. The shape of the bottle you use should give you inspiration. You can draw a design first on the bottle in pencil. Don't try to be too exact—the surface is quite slippery.

If the bottle will get a good deal of handling, give it a coat of Varathane or other plastic-base spray.

Shown in color on page 16

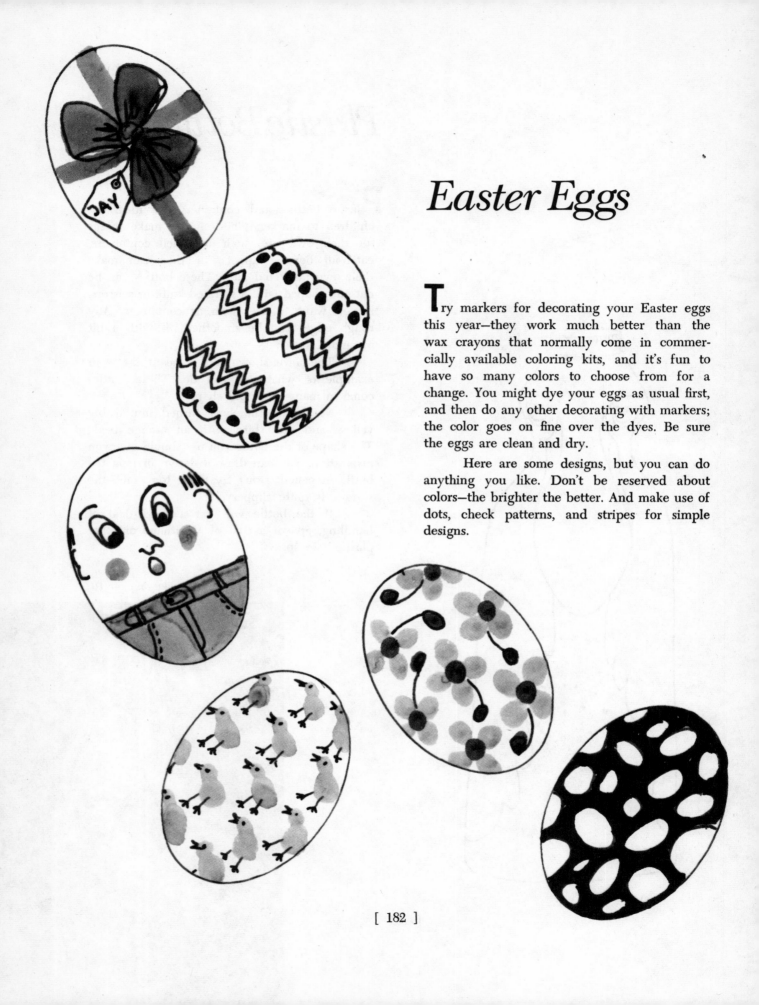

Easter Eggs

Try markers for decorating your Easter eggs this year—they work much better than the wax crayons that normally come in commercially available coloring kits, and it's fun to have so many colors to choose from for a change. You might dye your eggs as usual first, and then do any other decorating with markers; the color goes on fine over the dyes. Be sure the eggs are clean and dry.

Here are some designs, but you can do anything you like. Don't be reserved about colors—the brighter the better. And make use of dots, check patterns, and stripes for simple designs.

Moccasins

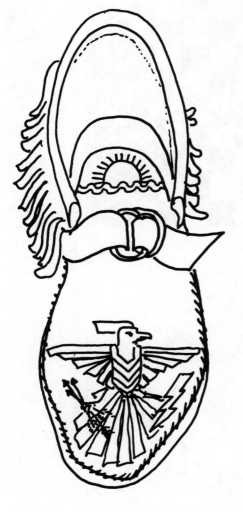

Markers on this buckskin suede look like sand paintings, and kids love them. The Indian Eagle motif looks very authentic; you can add more color by markering the fringe or the strap across the front. The same motif could be used on a small suede purse or wallet very handsomely.

The pattern for the eagle on the center front of the moccasin is given full size. You can transfer it with the carbon method. When working, stuff the moccasins with paper to give you support. We used a traditional American Indian color scheme—red, turquoise, ochre and brown.

Shown in color on page 16

Baby Blanket

Shown in color on page 16

This patchwork baby blanket is a labor of love, but it still doesn't take nearly as long as *sewing* a quilt, and it can be made a patch at a time at your leisure. The whole family might join in on a project like this, each person doing a square at a time. This blanket is 38″ x 42″ (87.5 x 105 cm.).

Quilted blankets like this one come with a pattern of stitching already in them, so you have a ready-made "grid" to follow. The sewn lines on this quilt determined the design itself. The patterns for many varieties of patches are given here and you can adapt them to your own quilt. You can also copy designs from other quilts.

The bleed of this synthetic fabric gave the traditionally crisp patchwork a pleasantly fuzzy effect. Unless the quilt will be used for purely decorative purposes, wash it before using it the first time to remove any possibly toxic traces of marker.

The quilt can probably be worked on as is; however, if you're using a ruler or templates, you may want to tack or tape the section of the quilt that you're working on to your work surface. There's quite a bit of small detail in some of these motifs, but you can transfer the main shapes to the quilt using the carbon method.

Our pale blue quilt is done almost entirely in various shades of blue, green, lavender and pink for a very soft look. The bright, mixed colors of traditional quilting would give a different but very pleasing effect.

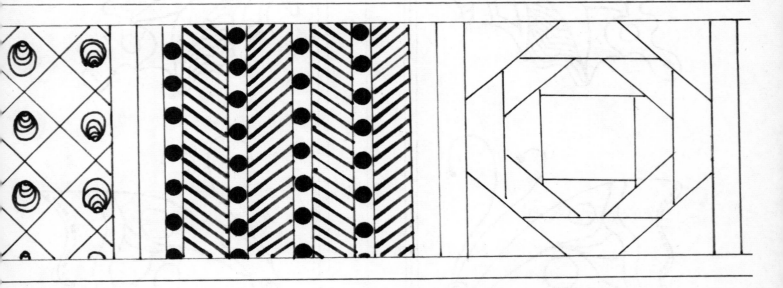

Child's Parka

Shown in color on page 16

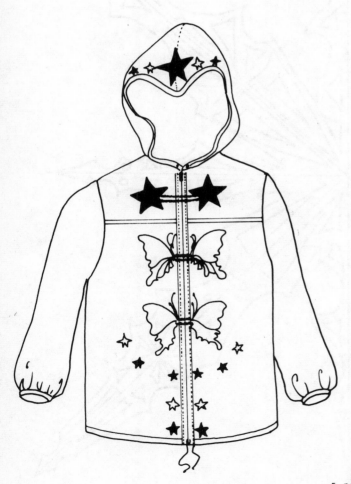

It was a pleasure to make this parka—the 100% nylon is a delightful surface to work on.

No special trick here; patterns are given for the butterflies and stars on the front of the jacket and for the snowflake on the back. Place them where they look best. On the front, zip up the jacket when laying it out. This way the butterflies will be level, and you'll make

sure they're properly spaced. For added interest, marker any detailing on the jacket such as plackets, ribbing, etcetera. If you're markering an old garment which has become worn, doctor up any dingy cuffs or worn places around the collar.

Use the carbon method to transfer your design. You can tape or tack the section of the parka you're working on to your work surface if it slips around too much. Be sure to put paper or cardboard between the layers while working to prevent the marker from bleeding through to the other side.

The entire design of this parka is outlined in black fine-line marker and colored in various shades of blue, with tiny touches of other colors. Stronger colors would be more appropriate for a boy's parka.

Child's Overalls

Shown in color on page 16

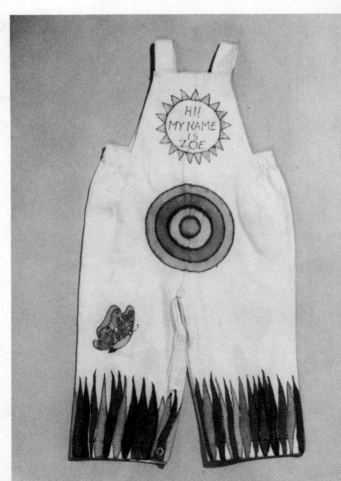

Zöe loves her "grass pants." Garments for small children are rewarding to do, because children's subject matter lends itself especially well to markers, and small garments take little time to complete.

Enlarge your pattern to the size you need and use the carbon method to transfer the design. To adjust the size, just add or subtract a little of the "grass" at the sides of the legs; the other motifs should be placed where appropriate. While working, place a piece of paper or cardboard between the layers to prevent the marker from bleeding. If you cut the cardboard to size, it can serve to hold the fabric on the legs of the overalls taut while working. Otherwise, tape or tack the garment to your work surface.

The grass motif is done in several shades of green, and the flowers and sun in reds and orange.

[189]

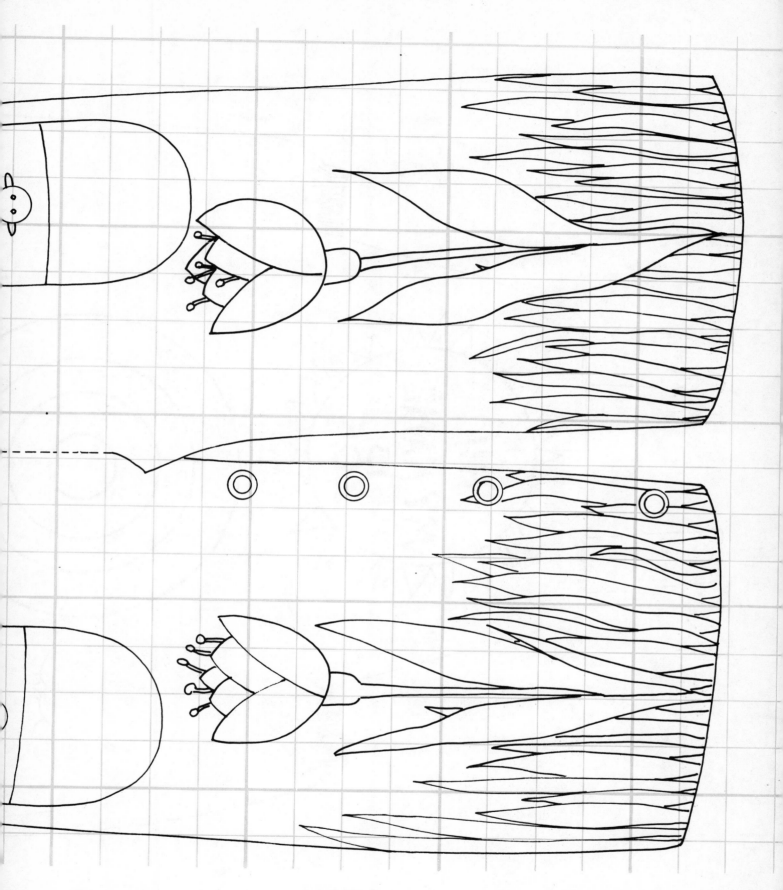

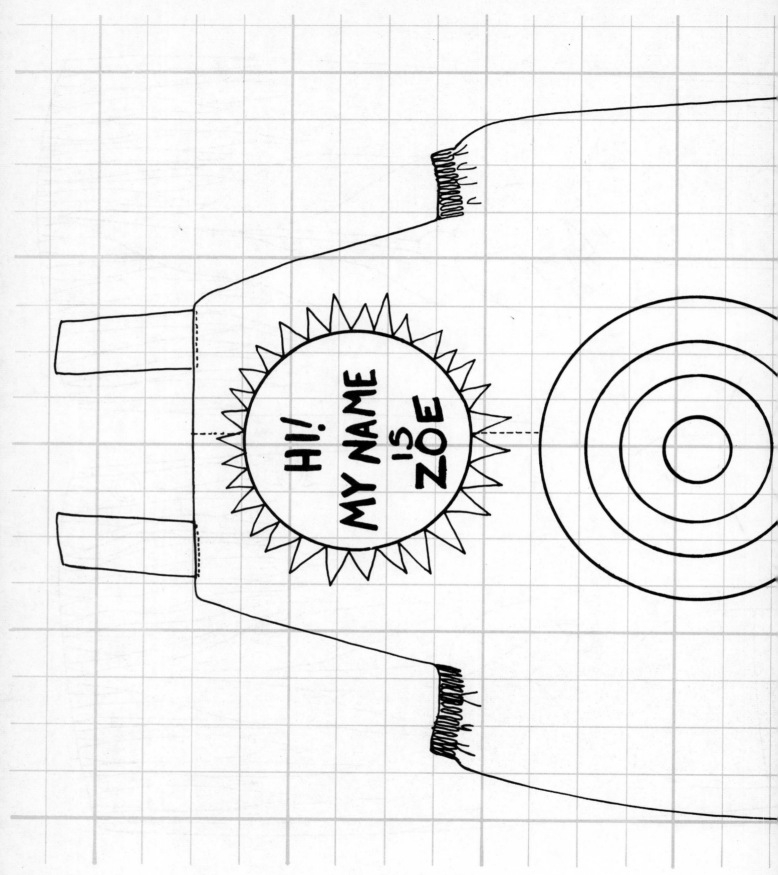

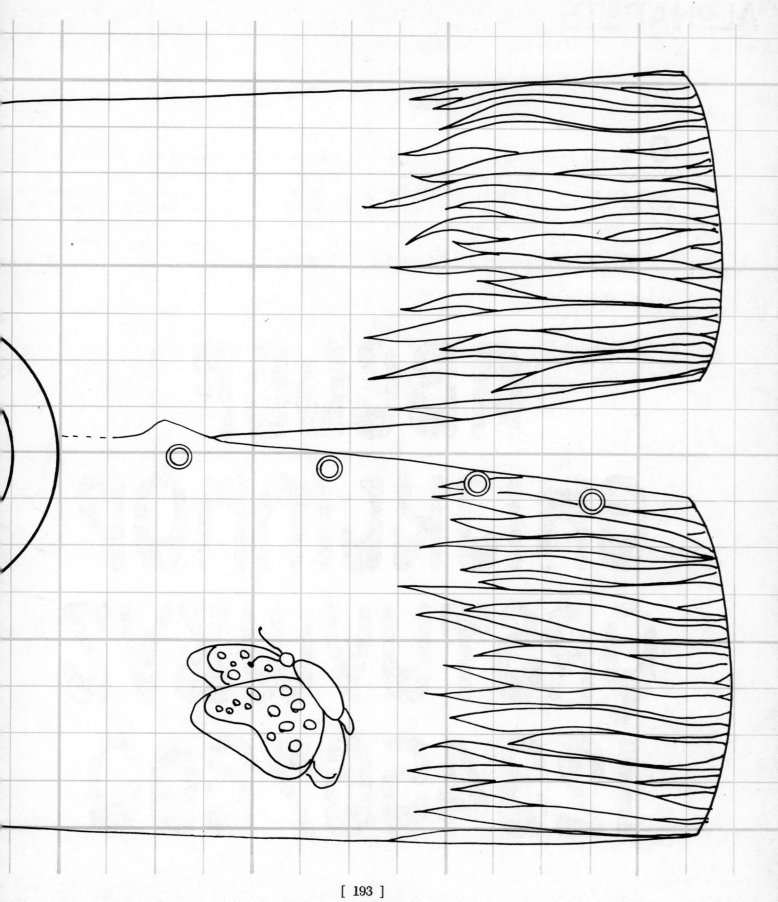

ALPHABETS

On the next several pages are some sample alphabets which you can use for monograms, names and messages on any of your projects. You don't have to copy all the detail if the style is too fussy or difficult; just the outlines of the letters would look very nice.

The alphabet on pages 196-197 could easily be done in two colors, with the solid area in one color and the dotted area another.

Transfer your message or monogram using the carbon method, enlarging the pattern if required. Don't forget, your own inimitable handwriting or lettering style is perfectly acceptable.

ABCDEF
GHIJKLMNOP
QRSTUVWXYZ
1234567890

AB
CDEFG
HIJKLM
NOPQRSSſſ
TUVWXYZ
¢%/£
&.:;!?'"''''~()*$
1234567890

ABC
DEFG
HIJK
LMN

O P Q R
S T U
V W
X Y Z

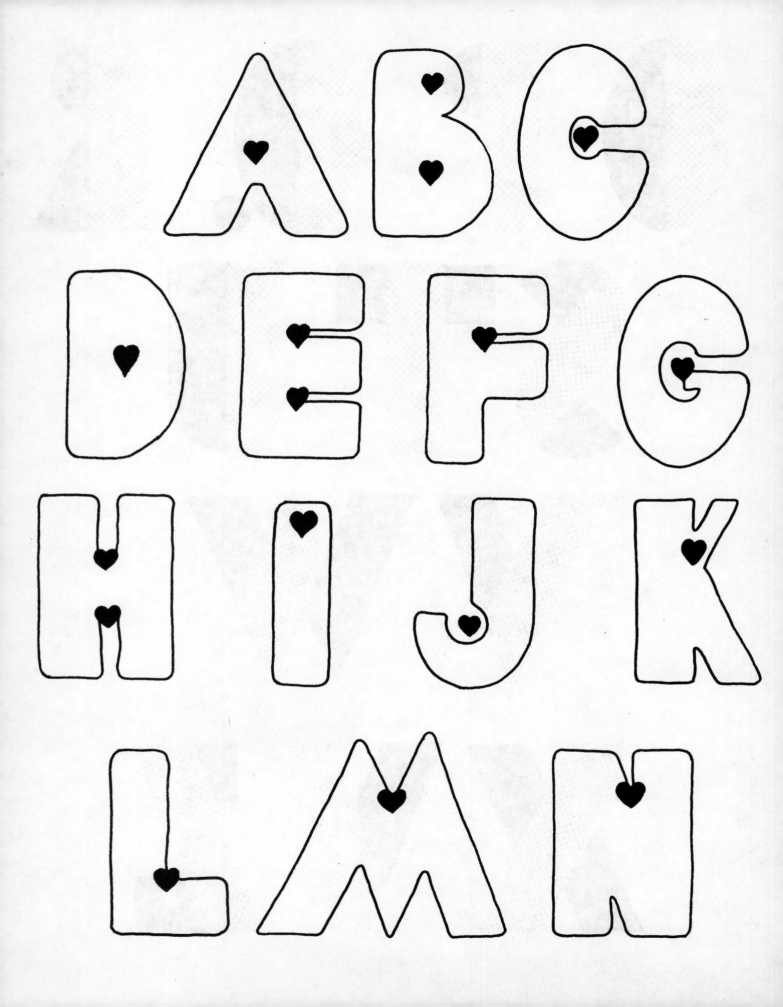

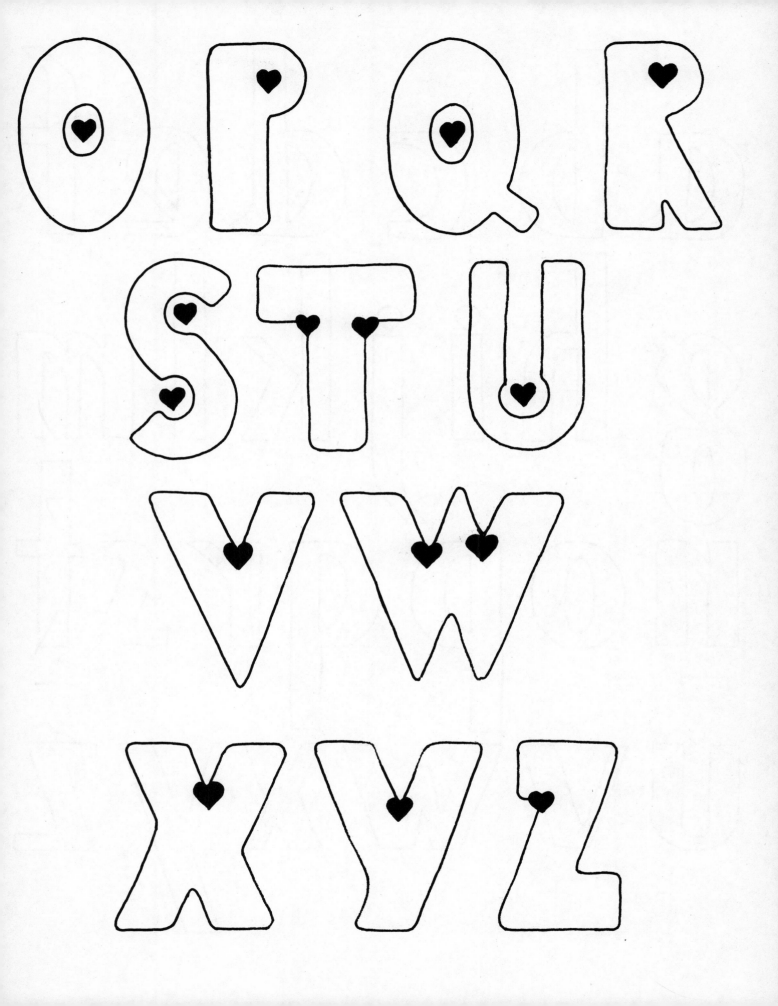

a b c d e f

g h i j k l m

n o p q r s t

u v w x y z